Write that book for the Glory
of God and the Good of people

Mother Teresa, 1990

The Camel
Knows the Way

A Journey by
LORNA KELLY

Published by Lorna Kelly
First Published in 1998
This book is currently available from:
Lorna Kelly
P.O. Box 1788,
Radio City Station
New York, NY 10101–1788

Cover photograph: Copyright
                    Carolyn Cowan
                    UK 0171-701-3845

ISBN 0-9664786-0-6

Library of Congress

Designed and printed by: CA Design
Rm 605–6 Kam Chung Building
54 Jaffe Road
Wanchai, Hong Kong

Dear Mary –
God bless you.

Lorna Kelly

January '99

Acknowledgements

It has been over ten years since I scrolled the first piece of paper into my typewriter to begin recording this journey. In that time there have been many souls who have woven in and out of my life, who have offered me their encouragement, their suggestions and their support. I thank you all.

Thank you Missionaries of Charity in all the corners of the world for your example of love and service and for giving me a story to pass along.

Thank you Nola Schiff for the hours and hours of editing. Thank you for your steadfastness with this project through many difficult times. I am blessed to have shared so many travels and travails with you.

Thank you Shep and Melba Brozman for being with me through so many years of the journey, for your love and support and for all the Sundays.

Thank you Lisa Hicks for offering your expertise, your insights and your unfaltering enthusiasm.

Thank you Annabel Davis-Goff for your time and for your invaluable help. Thank you for keeping me honest and for holding me to a standard.

Thank you Holly Clark for the intense eleventh-hour editing, for your daring. Thank you for reminding me to breathe during my dark night.

Thank you Tom and Kay Stretton for your generosity of spirit and for your consistent belief in me. Thank you for the help with commas and dashes, *et. al.* and etc.

Thank you Grossman, Brozman & Agrin for so generously allowing me to use your office during tax season.

Thank you Mindy Seeger, Jane Warrick, Sister Francita, Joe Argazzi, Irene Katz, Milton Rodriguez, Robert Callely, Gregory Gary, Richard Williams, Michael Carson, Richard Marcus, Rosie Stamp and Rosanne Chan.

Contents

The Camel
Knows the Way

Prologue

I was in the Sinai. I had been in Israel and crossed into Sinai to relax near the Red Sea for a few days. There was, a few miles from the small village where I stayed, an historical site I was interested to see. I could have gone by bus or taxi, but feeling adventurous, I decided to be Lawrence of Arabia and cross the desert. At the local market place I negotiated with a Bedouin to take me by camel.

The Bedouin introduced me to the kneeling creature, who assessed me from under hooded, bedroom eyes ringed with endless lashes. None too gracefully I climbed aboard and, following the Bedouin's instructions, placed my right calf around the pommel hooking my right foot behind my left knee. The Bedouin then gave a hissing signal and the animal lurched and swayed to its feet. The three of us—the Bedouin, the camel and I—set off into the desert. We were only about half an hour into the journey when the Bedouin suddenly handed me the reins and, in a combination of Arabic and broken English said, "The camel knows the way." Whereupon he slid off the animal's back and gave it a slap on the rump.

The camel ambled off with me ten feet in the air. Horrified, I swiveled in the saddle and shouted to the retreating Bedouin, "Where in God's name are you going? You can't leave me here. Come back!" I was scared of shouting too loudly, fearing that in camel language my words might mean, "Giddy-up. Full speed ahead." Whether the Bedouin chose to ignore me, or whether the wind made hearing me impossible, I'll never know. He simply disappeared over a dune.

I was panic-stricken. Here I was abandoned in the Sinai, an endless desert, not another soul or creature in sight, a prisoner a-top a camel whose name was not like that of other camels who had romantic Middle Eastern names like Rasheed, Ahmed, Kareem. No, my camel's name was Bob Marley.

My Lawrence of Arabia fantasies vanished. Instead I had visions of wandering for forty years, dying of thirst, or being ravaged by wild beasts. After a time I realized I simply had to calm down. What could I do? I was helpless. I gave up. In spite of my misgivings about the desert savvy of a camel with the name of a Jamaican reggae singer, I had no alternative but to trust the Bedouin's parting words.

As I swayed along in tandem with Bob Marley's soft plodding, I began to relax and feel comfortable with the rhythm of it all. And then I began to reason, "Well of course I'm in the Sinai. Isn't this where God brings all His chosen ones to commune with them? He spoke to Moses here, and did He not speak to Jesus in the desert one over from here? Or was that Elijah? Well, now I'm here so He obviously intends to speak to me."

I waited. . . .

Two hours later, Bob Marley delivered me to my destination. God had not spoken to me. I had received no message. *Except*, in short order, I had known the anticipation of adventure, the terror of abandonment, the desperation of helplessness, the exultation of spiritual grandiosity, the inevitability of surrender and, through it all, the simplicity of the journey.

Sunday,
March 15, 1981

It was early morning and already sweltering. The backs of my legs stuck to the taxi's leather upholstery and sweat tickled down my spine. Blasts of hot air pummeled my face as we hurtled along the roads at an outrageous speed— roads teeming with a multitude of men, women and children, walking, bicycling, balancing huge loads on their heads, herding goats and buffalo, pushing carts, or simply squatting on the side. Fertile fields and rice paddies flashed by intermittently in the scrubby landscape. I could scarcely register the speeding succession of images. This was a whole other world, startling, novel. This was Calcutta.

A gloomy, heavy haze clung to the city like a gritty shroud. I later discovered the haze was caused by traffic emissions and acrid smoke from thousands of small stoves dotting the sidewalks; it rose from the poor-quality coal and the pancakes of dried dung used for fuel—rose and hung in the atmosphere, trapped by the still, oppressive heat. Every surface looked grimy, every building, every canopy. Even the leaves on the trees were coated, weighed down by the thick gray deposit, giving them a sorry appearance.

In the city proper, my driver became even more frenzied. I was on the edge of my seat, clutching the window strap as we wove in and out of the crowds. How he avoided killing several pedestrians was a miracle, although it may have been due to the incessant blasting of the taxi's horn, which he applied even during rare moments when there was no one ahead of his vehicle. I berated myself for having chosen him out of the crowd of taxi drivers vying for my business at the airport. His gentle face and calm demeanor had fooled me; behind the wheel he was a madman.

We pulled up at the top of an alleyway off a busy main road. My driver pointed to a building on the corner and announced that we had reached my destination: 54A Lower Circular Road, the Mother House of the Missionaries of Charity founded by Mother Teresa. A statue of the Blessed Virgin, her hands together in prayer, looked down at me from a high niche on the side of the building.

I paid the fare and over-tipped, relieved at arriving undamaged. I retrieved my one small bag from the trunk and, still weak-kneed from the ride, entered the alleyway. About fifty feet along I came to a wooden door; on it was nailed a plain cross. On the wall next to the door a reversible sign read **MOTHER OUT** and, hanging through a hole in the wall, was a chain and handle. I pulled; on the other side I heard a bell ring. A few moments later the door opened.

Standing in front of me was a nun unlike any I had ever seen. For a moment we stared at each other across our separate cultures. The woman before me was Indian. She was wearing the habit of a Missionaries of Charity sister: a plain, white cotton tunic with mandarin collar and long sleeves. Over this was draped what looked to me like an oversized tea towel—a poor quality cotton sari bordered with three bands of blue, the outside band slightly wider than the other two. It was worn wrapped around the waist and over the head. On her head it was secured by straight pins to a white kerchief tied at the nape of the neck. On her left shoulder one corner of the sari was held by a safety pin from which hung a small crucifix. Her feet were bare.

I was dressed in Yves St. Laurent khaki culottes and a crisp, beautifully tailored shirt, well, perhaps not quite as crisp as it had been before the hectic taxi ride; my hands and feet were newly manicured and pedicured, my nails a brilliant Cadillac Red. Finally I broke the silence by breezily announcing, "Well, I'm here to help the poor!"

She smiled, no judgment registering on her face, and speaking in a soft, British English, invited me to enter. I stepped across the threshold into the courtyard of a large sprawling house that stood four stories high. Each floor had a balcony along one side overlooking the courtyard; in the far right-hand corner was a small grotto with a statue of Our Lady of Lourdes surrounded with potted plants all blooming in adoration. The nun directed me to a bench outside the parlor and asked me to wait for Sister Henry.

Sitting in the shade of the house, I was mesmerized by the goings-on around me. The yard was a hive of activity. About fifty young women, all wearing the same tea towel sari, were intently engaged in a variety of chores. Some pumped water by hand from a well at the far end of the yard; others, with sleeves rolled up, bent over metal buckets and vigorously scrubbed clothes with rough bars of soap. To avoid the wet ground, their saris and habits were hooked up into the cord around their waists, exposing their legs from the knee down—a sight I'd never witnessed in a Western nunnery. Others had whisk brooms and cleaned the yard with the discarded soapy water, sloshing it over the stone floor, directing it into gullies and drains. Many, regardless of their task, chomped on toothbrushes while they worked, their mouths white with foam. In India teeth cleaning is a strict part of personal hygiene, and a long time is devoted to the ritual each day. Half-curtains flip-flapped in doorways around the courtyard giving me an occasional glimpse of even more nuns in various rooms; still others were on the flat rooftop, hanging out yards and yards of freshly washed white gauze saris, turning the entire roof top into a Christo-like sculpture.

Not one of the nuns in the courtyard seemed to be at all impressed that I was fashionably dressed and my makeup perfect. Even though I must have appeared somewhat extravagant in this modest nunnery in the heart of Calcutta, ten thousand miles from my home in New York and light years from the life I had left just a few days before, I wasn't made to feel out of place. I knew by their joyful and welcoming demeanor that these women accepted me the same way they accepted all mankind, because they followed a Teacher who said, "Love one another; in this way people will know that you are mine." (John 15:12)

My life in New York was a long way away. It could not have mattered less to these women washing their clothes in a bucket that I was the first woman art auctioneer in America, employed by Sotheby's, the world's oldest art auction house. In New York I had what I thought to be a fascinating and enviable job and was considered to be an expert in a specialized area of Japanese art. I was earning a healthy salary, owned plenty of clothes and lived in a modest but perfectly contained apartment. I had valued friends and the respect of my colleagues and clients. My life was magical, better than I could ever have imagined. But just when I thought I held a winning hand, God threw in a wild card. My secretary, Lucille Defino, had given me a book called *Something Beautiful for God* by Malcolm Muggeridge. It changed the course of my life.

It had been an exhausting journey, full of upsets and irritations. Stopping in London had been trying; my mother was drinking and we'd argued. I had so much wanted a pleasant visit. The flight to Calcutta was filled to capacity, and behind me an infant had cried for hours. The child's desperate mother had borne the unkind stares; nobody had said anything, of course. I hadn't been able to sleep at all.

At first light the airplane was on approach to Calcutta. Staring through my window, all I could discern was a dense roof of palm trees streaked with a dark-blue mist; it gave the landscape a gloomy, prehistoric appearance. I half expected to see long-necked brontosaurs peering up out of the murky vegetation or pterodactyls swooping with snapping jaws in this alien, eerie world. The sense of destiny I felt so strongly when I began this journey had started to evaporate. I didn't feel quite so in sync with the universe. In fact, I began to feel a little unsure about the entire adventure.

After landing, we were instructed to remain seated until The Department of Health cleared us. We waited and waited inside the sweltering aircraft. At length the Department of Health did arrive—one skinny, barefoot little chap wearing a loose shirt and grubby knee-length khaki shorts, a leftover from the British. Holding aloft a can of disinfectant, he strode up and down the aisle spraying the cabin. This, we were told, was to prevent us from bringing any diseases into India. What lunacy! Here we were, spanking clean from the West, entering a filthy, overpopulated, poverty-stricken city frequented by cholera, typhoid, rabies, encephalitis and other diseases— and he was spraying *us!*

Spray hit my face. A nun was standing in front of me, apologizing. She had been sweeping a little too energetically and had whisked water onto me. Despite the fatigue assailing me, I felt exhilarated, perhaps because I had no idea what the next moment would bring; nor did it matter. I was acutely aware of physical sensations: the bench on which I sat, the floor under my feet, the cool of the shade, the glare of the sun in the courtyard, the scraping of brushes swooshing the soapy water into drains, the distant chatter of sisters in upstairs rooms. The moment crystallized, and I was bang in the middle of it. It was wonderful to be around nuns again; it felt familiar.

I was eight years old. Linda Briarley and I were running across the black and white marble squares in the foyer. Up the stairs past a statue of the Sacred Heart of Jesus—I forgot to touch HIS FEET and had to go back—we crept through a maze of corridors, halls and back passages. Linda came panting up behind me. "Lorna, Lorna, wait for me!" I waited impatiently for her at the top of the stairs; I only waited because she was my best friend. We went together, quietly, Linda and I, both in our winter uniforms: brown tunic over cream-colored blouse and a brown cardigan edged with blue and yellow stripes. No one was around. It was after lunch; the nuns were resting, and we were supposed to be in the playground. Linda was scared. I sensed her reluctance, so I took her hand and pulled her along the corridor.

More stairs and we were at a landing with a doorway. A forbidding, brown velvet curtain suspended from a brass pole shielded THE MYSTERY. I had often seen them go behind the curtain—Mother Agnes, Mother Frances, Mother Dorothy and all the rest—and I'd watched them come out again. I had once boldly asked Mother Angela what was behind the curtain. She had replied: "Curiosity killed the cat and gave the dog the measles."

So I had to know. Right before we parted the curtain, Linda stopped like a stone. "I don't want to," she said. When she said it, I hesitated, but I had to go in.

"All right," I whispered, "You guard."

Her eyes were huge in the shadowy corridor. I took a big breath and very, very cautiously pulled the heavy drape aside and tiptoed through.

On the other side of the curtain I could hardly believe my eyes. No wonder they kept it secret. It was Aladdin's cave. I had entered a wondrous mystical chamber. An exquisite private chapel painted a vibrant cobalt blue, a myriad golden stars gazing down from the domed ceiling. A holy, secluded retreat. Light from candle flames danced and sparkled and strained heavenward from multiarmed floor candelabra on either side of an altar. The room was filled with the scent of roses gathered from the convent gardens, lovingly arranged in ornate vases. And there, in the center of the altar, was the most beautiful statue of the Blessed Virgin I'd ever seen. Her long white dress, held about her waist with a golden girdle, hung in gentle folds brushing on the tops of her petaled bare feet. Over her dress she wore a blue cloak edged in gold, and the white veil covering her hair hung to her shoulders framing a perfect, angelic face. A halo of golden stars encircled the holy head.

I stood enthralled by the statue's beauty and gentle expression. The Blessed Virgin seemed to be looking right at me. I couldn't move. I was struck with wonder. The minutes passed by, maybe only seconds, before I noticed the black figure of a nun kneeling, her back to me. She must have heard me enter but, probably thinking I was another nun, didn't turn around. I dared myself to remain longer. My eyes greedily roamed the chapel, gobbling up every treasure.

The flames near the nun flickered suddenly, anticipating her move to rise from her devotions. Quickly I slipped like a fish into the waves of brown velvet. On the other side Linda had vanished. I heard voices. I looked about frantically, there was no way out. They came closer, their warm, soft voices preceding them. To my young eyes the nuns at Gumley were heroic, dignified, noble; I wanted to be one—a nun or a hairdresser, I wasn't sure which. But now there was no escape.

In a moment they wheeled around the corner, two of them, holy cowboys, their rosaries slung from the cinctures around their waists, swinging rhythmically against the flowing black, layer upon layer of fathomless black. I was transfixed. My heart sang with joy: "Who cares if I get punished? I don't care if I get punished. I've been behind the curtain. I know their secret."

They came nearer, Mother Perpetua and Mother Agnes. For a moment I panicked, hoping they wouldn't even notice me stock still in my brown uniform against the sea of brown velvet. . . .

"I'm sorry I kept you waiting. Welcome. I'm Sister Henry. May I help you?"

Sister Henry was Australian; I was surprised, I hadn't expected the sisters in India to be anything but Indian. She had fair skin and Frank-Sinatra-blue eyes. Her warm greeting relaxed me instantly. Her manner was gentle, cheerful and ladylike. I wasn't quite so ladylike, however, and after the initial pleasantries, bombarded her with questions about Mother Teresa. Sister Henry laughed putting her hand up to stop me. Mother was away on retreat she said, but was expected back in about five days, so if I waited, I could ask her all the questions myself. Again I was surprised. I had thought it might be complicated to actually meet with Mother Teresa, but Sister Henry assured me otherwise.

Since the Missionaries of Charity had no accommodation for outsiders, Sister Henry recommended I stay where many of the volunteers stayed—at the local YWCA. She invited me to return to the Mother House later in the afternoon for Adoration and then commandeered two diminutive novices to take me to the Y. These munchkins insisted on carrying my bag; it embarrassed me no end. I am almost five feet nine inches tall and, although my bag was not particularly big or heavy, the novices were so short they had to hold the handles up under their chins to prevent it from dragging on the ground. Between them they looked like a single mother cat carrying her overgrown kitten. I tried to take it away from them, but it was useless to protest. So, looking every bit a well-fed, well-clothed, privileged Westerner, I walked through the streets of Calcutta for the first time with two teeny, smiling, stumbling nuns beside me. It was an awkward introduction to this curious culture.

We edged our way through a maze of streets, so congested, so alive, so noisy and strange. Every imaginable thing was happening on those streets. The shops, scarcely more than grubby cubicles one on top of another, had open fronts where their proprietors sat on their haunches coaxing the passersby to look at their wares. We wove in and out of the crowds; beggars pulled at my sleeves; mothers held their babies out to me and beseeched, "*Baksheesh, baksheesh.*" The novices prodded me on, cautioning me not to give anything, because if I did, we would be surrounded.

On Rippon Street half-naked children played in the gutter; taxis, carts and other traffic passed by, alarmingly close. Although this was to be a common sight in India, I never quite got used to it. The children stopped and stared wide-eyed at us. Others came out of nowhere and skipped along at our heels—their hands out, smiling, giggling and pleading for coins or sweets. Despite their circumstances, they seemed to me to have the indomitable spirit of children everywhere. Babies with black kohl smeared around their eyes to protect against infection were carried by brothers and sisters scarcely bigger than themselves. None of them had shoes.

Rickshaws made their way through the crowds, their pullers fighting with the taxi drivers for space. There were slow moving, long-handled carts over-loaded with goods, pulled and pushed by skinny, barefooted workers. With the din of the horns, rickshaw bells, shouting men and roaring engines, it was mayhem. Men were sleeping on *charpoys* (beds made with ropes); how they slept with all the racket going on around them was a mystery. Older women squatted sedately on the curbs selling bunches of small bananas and oranges artfully arranged in circular straw baskets or some edible spicy mixture rolled and packaged in banana leaves. Everyone and everything had a place in the jumble of it all. What a city. So crowded, so polluted, so alive!

We arrived at the YWCA on Middleton Road. I was ushered by my companions into the office of Mrs. Moffat, a cheery, bespectacled Anglo-Indian who presided over the establishment. A room was available and after finances were settled, Mrs. Moffat provided me with two well-pressed gray sheets, a threadbare towel and a small padlock and key. On the second floor, I walked down a long, pleasant verandah overlooking tennis courts.

The room, or cell, that was to be my home for the next three weeks locked from the inside with a bolt and from the outside with the padlock and key. An iron-frame bed stood against one wall. On it drooped a lifeless mattress I dared not inspect too closely since I suspected I would not be sleeping alone. I covered the mattress quickly with the ancient gray sheets. Under the window stood a decrepit dressing table and a stool with a frayed wicker seat. A narrow closet was at the foot of the bed, and a painted wooden fan rotated slowly overhead.

The first thing I did was to give the house *wallah* a few rupees to clean the room, and then I ventured down the corridor to inspect the communal bathroom. The "bathroom" turned out to be a dingy, stone dungeon, its corners festooned with ancient cobwebs; the showerheads were rusty and the toilets seatless. I made a mental note to buy toilet paper, since it was obvious no luxuries of any kind were to be provided at the Y.

I unpacked my bag and went downstairs to the dining hall for lunch—an unpalatable mix of rice and watery *dal*; I was filled with foreboding about future meals at the Y. I started to feel the effects of jet lag and tried to resist since I was anxious to explore my new surroundings, but fatigue won and I collapsed on the bedraggled bed. I woke up a few hours later feeling refreshed and eager to join Sister Henry and the other sisters for Adoration. I ventured out and remembered my way back to the Mother House.

Adoration was an hour of prayer and meditation before the Blessed Sacrament. Each nun kissed the crucifix at the end of her rosary and made the Sign of the Cross. The congregation reaffirmed their vows of poverty, chastity, obedience and charity; the Mystery for meditation was announced and then the chant-like recitation of the Rosary began. Between each decade (ten Hail Marys) the nuns' voices swelled into song, feminine and sweet. Although I wasn't particularly interested in all this praying, I did want to be a part of the Missionaries of Charity experience, so I made up my mind to go along with whatever was presented. It was a pleasant and tranquil close to the day.

Afterwards, Sister Henry introduced me to some volunteers who were also guests at the Y. She quite surprised me by suggesting that I go to Kalighat the next day, to the House of the Dying to work with the sisters. I had come to Calcutta just as a curious observer, so the prospect of actually working side-by-side with the Missionaries of Charity was quite unexpected. I inquired what time the community began their day and was told the sisters said morning prayers at 5 am followed by Mass an hour later. I determined to join them.

I strolled back to the Y with the others. We had tea and sat on the verandah for a while, but my mind was reeling with the images of the day. I excused myself and went to bed. The traffic noise was still intense, but I had no difficulty falling asleep on the thin, lumpy pallet and scarcely noticed, nor cared about, the small creatures that did indeed share it with me.

Monday,
March 16, 1981

I woke up suddenly at three-thirty, disoriented in the unfamiliar blackness. An hour later I made my way along the corridor and downstairs. I was obliged to wake the night porter sleeping on a bench in the lobby. Not at all happy about being disturbed so early, he silently got to his feet and fished out a huge key from his pocket; he unlocked the door, pulled back the bolts and let me out.

It was exhilarating being up and about at that hour, passing through the city, sensing its collective heart sleeping, gently pulsating. I skirted the ranks of rickshaw drivers curled up under their carriages; I stepped around and over the ragged bundles of humanity covered with *kadi* cloth. Whole families were laid out like corpses on the pavements. Shadows flitted and shifted along the road ahead of me. In the morning gloom I could make out small children rummaging through the coals of yesterday's fires, searching for the few pieces not completely burned. Sounds of babies crying mixed with sounds of coughing and, from somewhere a few streets away, the sudden wail of a mullah over a crackling electronic megaphone reminding the faithful a new day was beginning. "All praise be to Allah."

Another early riser had just opened the shutter of the raised cubbyhole that was his shop and his home. He was brushing his teeth with a twig and ashes, spitting the dark foam into the street. We waved to each other but didn't speak. At a bend in the road I steeled myself to walk past a pack of mangy, sleeping dogs. Some of the filthy, lice-ridden curs woke up and barked, and others came right up and sniffed at me.

It was a twenty-minute walk from the Y along Rippon Street to Lower Circular Road. When I stood outside the wooden door of the Mother House, I hesitated; it felt unholy to be waking people at that hour. The bell chain was gone; it had been pulled inside, so I made a fist and pummeled hard. On the other side I could hear the two convent dogs barking and the slap of sandaled feet running toward the door; it was opened just wide enough for me to squeeze through. Inside, I crossed the courtyard and went up the stone staircase to the second floor. Outside the chapel, embedded in the cement on top of the balcony wall, was the holy-water font—an elliptical-shaped glass dish with a sponge in the bottom. I dipped my finger, made the Sign of the Cross and slipped off my sandals.

The chapel was a long rectangle with many shuttered windows on the far side overlooking Lower Circular Road. Centered just in front of this wall was the altar—a heavy, highly polished, dark wood table draped lengthwise with a lace-edged cloth embroidered with crosses. Mounted high on the wall behind the altar was a large crucifix with a typical nineteenth-century image of Christ in white plaster. There were splotches of blood around the piercings on his hands, feet and side, and blood dripped down his face from the thorn punctures on his brow; his loins were discreetly draped with an immaculate cloth. In plain black letters, stenciled directly onto the wall beside the crucifix, were the words **I Thirst**.

To the left of the altar was the lectern; to the right, a pedestal—on it stood a statue of the Virgin Mary poised on a half globe crushing a serpent beneath her bare feet. Further along, against the same wall, was the holy of holies—a golden tabernacle covered with a lacy veil, and next to the tabernacle, a candle burned in a red glass indicating the presence of the Blessed Sacrament. At either end of the chapel, to the left and right of the altar, was a blackboard; on it were chalked the Bible reference for the day, the Responsorial Psalm, the Communion song and the numbers of the hymns to be sung at Mass. Opposite the altar were three entrances to the chapel, and on the wall, between the doorways, were the obligatory fourteen small pictures depicting the Stations of the Cross. There were no pews or seats; the stone floor was covered with pieces of sacking material stitched together.

The nuns, a cloud of gauze in their white saris, moved past me in the early light and sat on the hard surface, their legs curled to one side. Dressed in the habit and sari of the Missionaries of Charity were over three hundred women silently awaiting the signal for morning prayers to begin; I was the only outsider. Sister Agnes, acting Superior in Mother Teresa's absence, patted the floor twice and the cloud rose and shifted to its knees. Prayers were recited from a small prayer book; each nun kept a stack of books of different sizes by her side: a larger prayer book, a Bible, and a hymnal, all covered with the same brown paper, reminding me of textbooks from my school days.

After prayers there was a twenty-minute silent meditation. Some closed their eyes; others fixed their gaze on the gory crucifix; some read. I was actually here *in Mother Teresa's chapel*, the very same chapel I had seen in pictures and read about in the book Lucille had given me for Christmas. In my meditation my thoughts drifted back and forth between recent events and the speed with which they had come my way.

Even though Lucille was well aware of my interest in the spiritual life, I still thought it rather an odd book for her to have given me. My life was too glamorous, fast-paced and important for me to read about a little nun doing good, living in some awful city on the other side of the world; I knew this nun had been awarded the Nobel Prize for peace, but that's all I knew. I had a deep interest in Jesus, but I had not applied much of his teaching to my daily life. I rarely read the front page of the newspaper to see what was happening in the world. I was like the man who, ignoring the headlines, flips immediately to the sports or business section. In my case, it was the arts section and, I'm afraid, the obituaries to scout for the possibility of forthcoming collections from the recently deceased.

I would have put the book aside indefinitely, but I was fond of Lucille and didn't want to hurt her feelings so, with an attitude of resignation, I skimmed through it while I had my coffee. As I read and looked at the pictures, my attitude changed. I became more and more intrigued. By the time I had finished the one hundred and fifty pages, I was fascinated by this woman whose entire focus was to serve God by helping the "poorest of the poor." Muggeridge explained how Mother Teresa's sole focus was to tend to the body of Christ as she saw Him "in the distressing disguise of the poor"—how her single mindedness and intense love had inspired thousands of young women to follow her in surrendering all their worldly goods and in devoting their lives to helping the "poorest of the poor" as Missionaries of Charity all over the world.

Often one comes across a word or phrase perhaps never encountered before, and quite suddenly, that same word or phrase seems to crop up all over the place—in crossword puzzles, magazine articles, conversation. So it was for me with the name "Mother Teresa." I'd scarcely heard of her. Now I heard and saw her name frequently.

A few weeks after reading the book, I happened to be in the mailroom at Sotheby's and overheard two clerks talking about a TV special on Mother Teresa of Calcutta to be broadcast that very evening at eight. I went home to my apartment, dragged the television out of the closet where it lived, and settled down to watch this woman about whom I'd heard so much. What I saw captivated me—a simple, down-to-earth nun much older looking than her seventy-odd years but radiating pure energy in the form of love. I was hooked by the woman and by her work.

The documentary showed dispensaries, food lines, the leper center, the home for the dying and the orphanages. I was intrigued that she had been able to build an organization on the spiritual basis of attending to the person immediately before her. Thirty-three years before, she had gone out onto the streets of Calcutta, picked up a dying woman lying in the gutter being gnawed by rats, and cared for her.

At the end of the program there was an interview with Mother Teresa. I was struck by her disarming directness and simplicity. I had to meet her. The next morning I called my travel agent and booked a round-trip ticket to Calcutta.

I was obliged to wait three weeks before departing; I had a contractual agreement to auction a collection of Japanese lacquer inro (small-compartmentalized boxes, about the size of a cigarette pack used for carrying snuff and medicines). It was an important sale: I had traveled to Arizona to select the pieces, had produced a dramatic catalog, had taken great pains over the research and every detail of the design, and I wanted to see the auction through.

It was a tremendous success. The cover piece sold for $50,000— a record. I felt wonderful and the seller was ecstatic. What a sendoff! I stepped out of the rostrum, went home, packed my bag, and the next morning took off for London to stay with my mother for a few days before continuing on to Calcutta. It had all happened so quickly and easily; I had a sense of being in step with my destiny.

Looking back at that time, I think God rendered me temporarily insane. If I had thought rationally, I probably would never have made the trip. I knew no one in India, and hadn't dared write to the Missionaries of Charity to say I was coming, knowing full well *they had no use for an auctioneer. I was afraid they would write back, "Unless you are a doctor or have some nursing skills, you should not come. But why don't you send us the money you intend to spend on your airfare, and we'll give it to the poor?" I had the complete dialogue running through my head, and, not wanting to be dissuaded, I decided I would just show up.*

Again Sister Agnes patted the floor twice to signal the meditation was over. And again the white cloud shifted to its knees. A bell rang, and padding along the corridor, preceded by a server, came a barefoot priest. The sisters sang. The priest kissed the altar, made the Sign of the Cross, and Mass began. By this time the city outside had stirred, and some of the volunteers and a few local people had come for Mass. A novice read the lesson in a voice impossible to hear above the din rising from Lower Circular Road. The priest shouted the gospel and a short homily. During the consecration of the host and wine, each kneeling nun bowed and touched her forehead to the floor. The Sign of Peace was the traditional Indian *namaskar*—the palms of the hands held together, fingertips touching the forehead in a slight bow.

Distributing Communion to the entire congregation took about fifteen minutes. I stayed sitting on the floor with my eyes lowered and watched the procession of bare feet and white cotton pass by; I got on the end of the line.

When Mass was over and the priest had padded out again, still more prayers were recited, among them the Saint Francis prayer beginning, "Lord make me an instrument of your peace." Followed by my favorite, the *Anima Christi*:

> Soul of Christ, sanctify me.
> Body of Christ, save me.
> Blood of Christ, inebriate me.
> Water from the side of Christ, wash me.

Passion of Christ, strengthen me.
O Good Jesus, hear me, within thy wounds hide me.
Suffer me not to be separated from thee.
From the malicious enemy defend me.
In the hour of my death call me
And bid me come unto Thee,
That with thy Saints I may praise thee.
Forever and ever. Amen.

Another beautiful prayer especially dear to the Missionaries of Charity: "Make us worthy, Lord, to serve our fellow men throughout the world who live and die in poverty and hunger. Give them through our hands, this day, their daily bread, and by our understanding love, give peace and joy. Amen."

Finally, four verses from a hymn honoring the Blessed Mother were recited, and the morning devotions finished with "Mary, cause of our joy, pray for us," and the Sign of the Cross. The white-draped congregation filed out, each clutching her stack of brown books. It was 7 am. Sister Henry came over to ask if I was settling in all right. I assured her I was fine.

I headed back to the Y for breakfast. The streets now were jammed with traffic and people. The shrouded bundles that had been on the pavements a few hours before were gone—transformed into workers, beggars, and rickshaw drivers. I stopped to watch a man and a child, I presumed his son, sitting cross-legged in a teeny kiosk making *bidis*— slim cigarettes of tobacco rolled in a kendu leaf and tied with cotton thread. Holding one end of the thread in their teeth, the other in their toes, the two produced the *bidis* with astonishing speed and deftness and then arranged them in neat piles ready for sale.

After breakfast I caught a bus to Kalighat with Trudi,

one of the volunteers. The bus was packed and leaned precariously as we went around corners at top speed. The interior was gaily painted, rather like a gypsy caravan; a framed picture of Krishna bedecked with garlands hung at one end in the women's section.

Having a women's section on the crowded bus seemed an incongruous courtesy caught in the harsh life and frenzy of the city. A length of string ran from the back of the bus up to the driver's cab and served as the bell pull. Despite the congestion the conductor managed to squeeze himself up and down the aisle, collecting fares and handing out different colored tickets.

No one was reading a newspaper (paper goods are expensive in India), and so Trudi and I became the main attraction for the rest of the passengers. We did look rather unusual in this crowd—both tall and fair, me with long red nails and lipstick, she with white-blonde hair cut extremely short.

Trudi was from Austria; she had been in Calcutta for six weeks working with the Missionaries of Charity and intended to stay on for another month. She told me the work could be physically and emotionally exhausting and suggested I take it easy for the first week. She also warned me to take my malaria pills since a few of the volunteers had come down with malaria, and the ensuing fevers were not a pleasant experience.

Twenty minutes on the bus—then we had to push, squeeze and struggle to get off. We were in a bustling marketplace. Trudi explained that for Hindus, Kalighat is sacred, the focal point of the area being the Temple of the goddess Kali. The bloodthirsty Kali is also regarded as the benevolent mother, kind and compassionate, concerned for her children. Mad-eyed effigies of the deity wearing a necklace of snakes and skulls abounded in wall niches, on stalls, on cards and hangings. The bazaar around the temple was a jumble of stalls, noises, people, smells. Vendors selling talismans and relics to assist in devotions to Kali shouted out their wares. Women sellers squatted amidst a profusion of tiny buds and flower heads of roses, jasmine and marigolds, all of which they skillfully strung into delicate garlands to be offered at the temple. The fragrance of the flowers mixed with the pungency of incense wafting over the market evoked a sense of being caught up in an exotic fairytale.

Adjoining the temple of Kali was the Missionaries of Charity's home for the dying, Nirmal Hriday (Bengali for Immaculate Heart)—simply called Kalighat by the sisters. Opened by Mother Teresa on August 22, 1952, Nirmal Hriday was her first center and held a special place in her heart. Once the resting-place for pilgrims visiting the Kali Temple, it is now a hospice where the sisters tend to the outcasts, the helpless, the unwanted and the dying. "I have lived my life like an animal, but I will die like an angel," declared one old man who had been brought in off the streets.

We entered a large building divided into two dormitories—one for the men, the other for women. Near the entrance was a photograph of Mother Teresa with the words "Mother's First Love."   There were many simple religious pictures on the walls. A small office area housed the supplies cabinet and the desk of Sister Luke, a trained nurse who was in charge of the hospice.

When Mother Teresa first opened the home, she endured the animosity and threats of the locals who were convinced the Missionaries of Charity were evil women converting dying Hindus to Christianity. Stones were thrown, windows broken. At one time Mother Teresa herself faced a dangerously hostile mob and stood her ground. "Kill me," she dared them. "I don't care, it will only mean I will be with God in Heaven all the sooner."

The locals called the Chief of Police to drive out the Missionaries of Charity. After touring the hospice and seeing for himself Mother and the sisters feeding and tending to the broken bodies of the patients, he faced the crowd. "I will close this center down," he promised, "just as soon as you can get your mothers and your sisters here to do the work this woman is doing." The harassment stopped immediately.

Each dormitory housed over sixty metal cots with green plastic-covered mattresses. On either side of a central passage was a row of cots with another row on a raised stone platform. Along one wall, small arch-shaped windows shed a dim light across the pale green walls. At the far end of the dormitory was a stone washroom. The place looked dismal—smelled dismal—and felt dismal.

I walked among the low cots in the women's section and saw the human wreckage lying there. The sights were so wretched that an unconscious protective mechanism detached me from my feelings. Some appeared a thousand years old—wrinkled, calcified and curled in the fetal position. Others were clearly young, but near-starvation had prematurely aged them. Some were in terrible pain with enormous open sores on their shriveled bodies. Still others had been so brutalized from years of living on the pitiless streets that they were mad. Some had TB. Others were simply dying.

Trudi handed me a large blue apron and asked me to help with the bathing. Patients would either walk or be carried to the back room to be washed down in luke warm water, dried and dressed in clean robes. I stooped over a bag of bones, once a woman. She was covered in wrinkled, paper-thin skin that was stretched so tautly over her frame it looked as if it might easily split. As I washed her and rinsed her off, she whimpered ceaselessly. The old towel used for drying was so rough, I was fearful of tearing her skin. I put the clean gown on her still-damp body; the day was already so hot she dried in minutes. When I carried another woman into the washroom, fat white maggots plopped out of the festering wound on her buttock and wriggled on the floor. I felt sick.

I worked the morning away doing things I never dreamt I'd be doing. After the bathing, I tended a bedridden patient who could not have weighed more than sixty pounds. Her arms and legs were sticks protruding from an emaciated torso. Her breasts had long since gone. Her dark skin was mummified and brittle, like some unbandaged defunct pharaoh. On her bony hip was an enormous pustule and bloody bed sore that bore right through to the bone; there was no way her defeated body could ever heal it. Sister Luke gave me some cleaning liquid. I swabbed as gently as I possibly could into the dying flesh but had to look into her brown eyes staring back in helpless agony and listen to the low moaning issuing from her wracked form. When I finished, I stroked her fuzzy head for a moment or two, touched her sunken cheeks. I could feel the tears burning my eyes; I turned to deal with the next case.

I dressed more bedsores, cleaned up vomit and excrement, and fed those too sick to feed themselves. The feeding was a slow process; it was an achievement to get even the meagerest morsel into their systems. After one tiny spoonful it felt like an age before they'd finished chewing and were ready for the next. Patience not being one of my strong suits, I found this feeding an exacting, somewhat irritating exercise.

At midday the sisters and volunteers left the hospice. The sisters returned to the Mother House for lunch and a short rest, the volunteers returned to the Y. I was truly spent by the work, the heat, and the time difference. I decided to take Trudi's advice and go easy for a few days, or else I feared I would end up on a cot in Kalighat myself. It was incredibly hot; the diet was not at all nourishing. I would have to be careful.

Tuesday,
March 17, 1981

Leaving the Mother House after Mass, several of us stopped at a dairy, a tiled shop that had large pails of milk and giant earthenware jars of yogurt. Both the sweet and the sour curd were delicious. I ordered a portion of the sweet; it was scooped into a small earthenware crock, covered with a square of grease paper and secured at the neck by a rubber band. My companions said they ate yogurt every day, that it was a good liner and a deterrent against stomach bugs. I decided to call at the dairy every morning; I certainly needed some defense against the Y's food, which was bound to do me in eventually.

The gutter near the dairy was littered with broken clay; Brahmin dietary law required each crock be smashed after consumption of its contents. There were no bins or trashcans in sight; all waste was thrown into the gutters. How it was swept away I wasn't sure, but there appeared to be an efficient garbage service in Calcutta, greatly abetted by the garbage pickers. The crows and the rats played their part too.

I returned to Kalighat with Trudi. The first task of the day was to serve breakfast: a banana, a slice of bread and puffed rice on a tin plate and, ladled out of a metal pail, a mug of milky tea. No one used spoons or forks. Every patient ate with her fingers. Again I had to endure the long process of feeding the helpless. While I waited for them to chew each mouthful agonizingly, my gaze wandered around the room. I watched another volunteer. She seemed to be doing the feeding with love, concentration and patience. What did she see in all this that I didn't? Another volunteer was attempting to coax a blanketed lump to eat—an old woman had rolled herself up in a cat-like ball so it was not easy to tell where her head or feet were; there was just a soft wailing coming from under the cover.

The hospice was kept spotlessly clean, swept and washed down several times a day, but no matter how thorough our efforts, we could not rid the place of the sickly smell of excrement and putrid flesh. Frequently the ancient patients would get off their cots, squat on the floor, and defecate. The unholy stench which arose could nearly always be tracked to one of these bedside packages.

After breakfast the patients were washed, the bedding on the cots changed, dressings applied, and medicines distributed. By then it was around eleven o'clock and time for lunch. Lunch was the same as the day before: rice with *dal* ladled out of the same large pails onto tin plates with a mug of water to wash it down.

The enormous kitchen on the premises looked like a witch's hearth with cauldrons hanging and hissing over open fires. Squatting in the middle of the room was a group of chattering women, peeling and chopping vegetables. One woman washed out the huge pots in floor-level sinks, while others pounded at the laundry in steaming vats nearby. Standards at Kalighat were certainly different. One of the cooks was a leper, her face deformed and some of her fingers missing, but in Kalighat all hands were welcomed, fingers or no.

Some of the kitchen workers were permanent residents of the hospice; they had been taken in off the streets, had recovered, and stayed on. One mannish, deep-voiced woman, who suffered with elephantiasis, told me she had been at Kalighat over eight years and hadn't been outside since she arrived. Another, Hazel, was a woman-child; I figured her to be over forty but it was difficult to tell. She was small and had a girlish body; she had the voice and mannerisms of a little girl: her hair hung in two schoolgirl braids; she wore a little girl's frock with puffed sleeves and a sash tied in a bow at the back, and she adorned herself with masses of plastic jewelry. Despite some obvious mental disorder, she was bright and agile, and her English made her an invaluable interpreter. I suspected she had known better days. Hazel, too, seemed content to spend the rest of her life in the house of the dying.

Kalighat served as a place of last resort for the destitute: the old, the sick, the dying, the unwanted were brought to this clean, quiet haven and loved. Most died. When death occurred, the nuns would wrap the body in a sheet and take it to the morgue, a blue-tiled room off the kitchen. The room had two shelves to hold the bodies and a slowly rotating overhead fan. A sign on the wall proclaimed **I AM ON MY WAY TO HEAVEN**.

When I looked in, both shelves were occupied; on the lower shelf lay a very thin bundle, tied at both ends like a Christmas cracker, and on the top shelf, a tiny wrapped bundle. With a shock I realized it was a child. I stood in the room for several moments feeling confused. This was outside my range of experience. I hadn't seen any children in the hospice. I wondered about this child. Did the parents bring it in? How did they cope with their loss?

Pamela was my sister, my parents' firstborn. When Pamela was three years old, she contracted meningitis and died within four days.

It was a terrible blow to my young parents. They were advised to "go in for" another child immediately to help them forget the dead one—a common solution in those days. There was no accommodation made for the mourning process; therapy of any sort was unheard of; besides, it was wartime and many families were suffering with painful losses. Ten months after Pamela died, my brother Sean was born. I arrived four years later.

Although my parents never held Pamela up to me as a model, the message came through in subtle ways. Relatives would reminisce about her, "What a darling and beautiful child." "What a good girl."

It was painfully obvious to me that Pamela had been too good for this world and that God had taken her into the next. On the dresser in my parents' bedroom, sat an oval framed picture of her—soft, fair curls forming a halo around the permanently smiling angelic face. People said her sweet disposition matched her sweet looks. There was no way I could measure up. I was blonde, yes, but my hair was straight and hung in a heavy curtain around my head. My eyebrows held hands over the bridge of my nose, giving me a glowering, bad-tempered look. And, indeed, I was bad-tempered at times. I had a secret fear that I didn't really belong to my parents, that I was a stranger in the house, and that as soon as they discovered their mistake, I'd be packed off.

My brother seemed to be my mother's delight. He was rarely told off or walloped for misbehaving. He suffered with asthma, and I suffered whenever he had a severe attack; I would stand outside his bedroom door while the doctor visited, praying fervently to God not to let him die. If he were dead, he would be eternally perfect, just like Pamela, secured in a little oval frame on the dresser.

I shut the door of the morgue.

When all the patients had been served their lunch, our duties ended. We wandered back through the bazaar, drinking in the atmosphere—dazzlingly colorful saris, jewelry, flowers, fruits, utensils, spices, grains—all was vibrating with life and flavor. I stopped in front of the flower-threading women and bent down to pick up one of the garlands. Trudi stopped me, cautioning me not to touch unless I intended to buy, because once I'd touched a garland, it would be considered religiously contaminated. I had so much to learn.

We dallied at the bazaar for an hour or more. Lunch was cold when we got back to the Y, but hot or cold made no difference—it was still ghastly. Breakfast at the Y was the only passable meal; it usually consisted of tea, an egg, some toast, jam and a couple of small bananas. This very morning I had wanted some extra toast, and seeing none of the waiters in sight, I followed my nose and entered the kitchen, which was strictly "out of bounds." No one was there. I pursued an aroma of burning bread through the kitchen to the back yard. There, in the middle of the courtyard, surrounded by the waiters, was a half-naked man squatting on his haunches, holding a twig with a piece of bread on the end of it, turning it over a small fire.

After lunch I took a long shower, scrubbed the soles of my engrimed feet and wondered if they would ever be clean again. I read for a while, took a nap, then made my way back to the Mother House for Adoration.

Looking around at the nuns in the chapel, I felt a twinge of envy at their faith. They appeared so absorbed in their prayers. I marveled at how still they stayed, kneeling on the stone floor with just a thin layer of sacking between their knees and the hard surface. My knees killed me, and I constantly had to shift my weight or sit back on my haunches. It was not easy to get into a mood of adoration with pain shooting through my knees. I indulged in thoughts of Gumley again.

The house itself was beautiful. An early nineteenth-century description read, "The entrance hall was paved in squares of black and white marble, with a wide, oaken, parquet staircase and ceilings painted by Sir Godfrey Kneller, representing scenes from heathen mythology. Pleasure grounds of six acres surrounded it, laid out in one part as a shrubbery and plantation of trees, while in another were the vegetable garden and in the center a considerable piece of water and a green paddock."

The Faithful Companions of Jesus, the teaching order that ran Gumley, acquired the house in 1841 and, I am sure, promptly did away with the heathen mythology on the ceiling, for no good Catholic girl should have her eyes corrupted by such sensational scenes. Instead there were religious paintings and statues throughout, conducive to a serene, meditative and Catholic atmosphere. The "piece of water" had been filled in for the safety of the students, but every year, as if heeding some ancestral memory, ducks came to the lawn where the lake had been and nested in the shrubbery. The few acres at the back of the house were our magical playground and all that remained of the original park.

My very favorite place, however, was the school chapel. There was so much for the eyes to feast upon—statues of the Holy Family and various saints and angels, evocative paintings of biblical scenes and soul-stirring Stations of the Cross. A golden altar rail separated the congregation from the sanctuary, and painted in gold on the molding high above the altar were the words "Sanctus, Sanctus, Sanctus." I loved being alone in that special place. I liked the silence, the holiness, and in my childlike way, I loved God. It was there at the age of seven, in white dress and veil, I made my First Holy Communion, careful not to let my teeth touch the host in case I accidentally took a bite out of Jesus.

I loved the nuns at Gumley. It was impossible to think of them as ordinary women. I was especially intrigued by their complicated habits; I could never tell which bit went where or how they ever got *into all those layers that showed not a smidgen of flesh except face and hands. A wisp of hair that sneaked out from beneath the wimple would be enough to keep me entranced all day long. I thought their habit magnificent. To be perfectly honest, I think my desire for religious life was chiefly motivated by a desire to swathe myself in the garb. After Vatican II, when nuns took to more modern attire, my desire for consecrated life evaporated.*

I was also intrigued by their hidden, private lives. I had a burning curiosity about really important things: for instance, what was their hair like? What did they wear to bed? Were they allowed cozy underwear? Did they ever see their mothers? What went on in their private refectory? A million questions.

That night back at the Y, I ate the evening meal, a deep-fried vegetable concoction, and silently gave thanks for the morning yogurt. I sat on the verandah chatting with the volunteers, most of whom had been in Calcutta for a couple of months and knew the ropes. The good company and shared pleasantries brought on an agreeable sleepiness, and I was in bed by nine.

Wednesday,
March 18, 1981

Walking back to the Y after Mass, my attention was caught by great lumps of gray meat and split carcasses of sheep and goats hanging in the open-air butchers' shops. Seeing the dead flesh covered with flies, I couldn't imagine anyone actually bought the dreadful-looking stuff to eat. Yards and yards of entrails spilled over the edge of the stalls into a pile on the street. A butcher was sorting through the slimy intestines while, just out of arm's reach, a semi-circle of dogs attentively watched his every move.

In the many tea stalls, the tea *wallahs* squatted beside their *chulas* (stoves). The kettle, or saucepan, of sweet milky tea was brought to the boil, and the mixture was then poured, with a great flourish, from a height of a few feet to make it froth in the small glasses. Sometimes, in the more classy establishments, seating for the customers was provided in the form of a plank of rough wood supported by bricks.

In another cubicle, a tailor, scissors in hand, knelt on a piece of cloth that covered the entire floor of his tiny shop. His partner, squeezed into a corner, operated an ancient Singer sewing machine with a foot treadle. The vegetable seller's stall barely contained the seller, let alone two-dozen tomatoes, a few bunches of bananas and a handful of potatoes. The candy store was a niche in the wall—the owner sold boiled sweets, a yellow milk candy made from chickpeas and condensed milk, and *Barfi* (Bengali nougat coated in thin silver paper), all stored in grimy glass jars on a makeshift shelf.

I was drawn once again to the tobacco kiosks and watched the *bidi* makers. Soft drinks and cigarettes were also sold at the kiosks; cigarettes were rarely purchased by the pack but more likely one or two at a time. The briskest business, however, was the sale of *pan*, an addictive stimulant of tobacco, chopped betel nut, chutney and cardamom placed on a betel leaf smeared with white lime paste. The leaf is then folded into a tight cone-shaped packet and fastened by means of a clove poked through flaps of the shiny leaf—it is a great favorite in India, and many older men and women had red-stained mouths and decaying teeth from chewing it. I had wondered what all the blood-like blotches on the streets, walls and sidewalks might be until I realized they were caused by the *pan* chewers' spit.

Each customer has his or her *pan* rolled fresh, and the skill with which the ritual is performed matches that of the *bidi*-making process. I noticed Indians, in general, used their hands in a particularly mesmerizing way. They expressed themselves with artistry of movement not unlike the intricate gestures employed in classic Indian dance. The *pan* makers, the tea *wallahs*, the *roti* cooks, the flower threaders, had a similar extravagant style; it was fascinating to watch. Even the ticket collectors on the buses, like croupiers in the finest casinos, had a snappy routine; they held the tickets in between each finger theatrically flicking them over while making change.

On Rippon Street school children wearing English uniforms—white shirts and striped ties, the boys in short gray pants, the girls in gray skirts—were grouped around the school gate. The more affluent children arrived by rickshaw, accompanied by their servants. I stood and watched a group of girls tease one of their companions, circling her, talking and laughing loudly. The object of their taunts clutched her satchel to her chest and fixed her eyes on the ground.

"She's ever so posh don't yer know. Go on, say something then."

They were moving around and around me, Doreen and Priscilla and the others. I remained silent. "Go on. Go on." I felt someone poking me in the back. "Say something why don't yer?" Doreen's voice was shrill near my ear.

"What do you want me to say?"

A shriek of triumph! They nudged and elbowed each other and trilled, "Oh she's ever-so lah-de-dah."

I'd had to leave Gumley. I'd failed my Eleven Plus, a compulsory examination taken by all eleven-year-olds in England; its results determined their academic future. I was unable to go on to the senior school at Gumley and was sent instead to Marlborough Secondary Modern School for Girls. I felt a terrible sadness when I wheeled my bicycle out of the front gate of Gumley for the last time.

At Marlborough I heard swearing and talk of sex. My classmates were a rough crowd of girls compared to the white-gloves-and-Panama-hat set I'd been used to. I had a cultured voice and was soon the victim of their taunts. I tried to change in order to fit in. I started constructing a protective front.

In Calcutta it seemed all of life happened in full public view. Bathing is part of Hindu ritual, and no matter what the temperature, the men gather at the water pumps wearing only their *longhis*—a length of fabric wrapped around their lower bodies like a skirt. With skillful modesty, they vigorously soap, scrub and then rinse off by using anything handy to pour water over themselves from head to foot. Men urinating in full public view, however, took a little getting used to. I came across a couple of them squatting and peeing against a wall—they don't usually stand as Western men do. The other volunteers laughed at my reaction; they were already used to it and I became used to it too. I never saw a woman crouching in the streets. I had no idea when they tended to their bodily functions—probably earlier, I guessed, in the obscurity of dawn.

After breakfast I walked with Blondine to Prem Dan. Blondine was one of a group of French volunteers; she had been in Calcutta a month and had made the hospital at Prem Dan her base. It was a forty-five minute walk from the Y; everything was horribly rundown; not one traffic light worked. At every screaming, chaotic intersection, a policeman in dingy whites stood on a small wooden podium, or on a larger, concrete circular island, attempting, at great risk to life and limb, to control the cacophonic flow. The pavements that once must have been wide smooth walkways were now cracked and broken. Many of the stone slabs were missing altogether.

We passed several pitiful young girls sitting in the middle of the sidewalk, nursing babies. One of them, with a Madonna-like face and a baby at her breast, could only have been a child herself, maybe fifteen years old. Blondine gave her a banana saved from breakfast. The young mother in turn offered Blondine the traditional *namaskar* and the most captivating smile. I determined to follow Blondine's example.

There were family groups at various street corners sitting on scraps of sacking. Naked babies crawled on the sidewalk under the watchful eye of adults who were talking among themselves and eating meager portions of rice out of tin bowls. Despite the wretched conditions, there was an air of everyday normality about the scene.

We crossed an intersection at Park Circus and walked up a slight hill passing shacks made of woven straw, sheets of plastic and other discarded material. The huge black water pipe that ran along the length of the hill was coated with dung patties used for fuel. Children were making them by taking the moist dung and, with the same skill, deftness and concentration the *bidi* maker had displayed, forming the little patties in their hands and slapping them onto the pipe to dry. They stopped and watched us as we passed.

Prem Dan had once been a factory owned by the British company ICI. When the company pulled out of Calcutta in 1975, the owners turned over the whole huge complex to Mother Teresa. The entire compound was surrounded by a high wall and sprawled across nearly two acres next to the Tiljala railroad station. We crossed a bridge over the tracks and entered Prem Dan through a door in the wall. The gateman stationed within bowed and scraped as he ushered us through; then in a flash, he changed into a raging bully, shouting and bossing the people who were gathered outside the entrance and came every day for food and medicine.

We were now in a foul-smelling yard where people squatted on their haunches, beating coconut pulp and stripping husks for straw matting. They halted their pounding to raise their hands in the *namaskar*; we returned the greeting. Close by was a stockade for pigs—the source of the pervasive ripe odor. A little way along a brick path was the hospital itself, if one could call it a hospital, comprised of two hangar-like buildings divided into men's and women's sections with a chapel sandwiched between.

Blondine introduced me to Sister Ursha, the Superior, and then departed to start her duties. Sister Ursha was probably in her early thirties; a sweet, delicate woman, she had a huge responsibility overseeing the administration of Prem Dan, and although she was busy, she took the time to show me around. The first stop was the nursery section, where children under the age of five were housed. They were jumping up and down in their cots, playing, crawling, running, squealing, screeching, crying, chirping; I couldn't stop grinning at their antics and the delightfulness of it all. I could have stayed with them all day, but Sister Ursha didn't want to dally, so we moved on to another section where women were learning to sew on the same type of ancient Singer sewing machines I had seen in the tailor shops.

In another room typing lessons were in progress. The typewriters were of the same vintage as the sewing machines—upright manuals with circular black keys. We then moved on to a classroom where children were having a geography lesson. When we entered, they scrambled to their feet and chanted, "Good morning, Sister; good morning, Madam." Sister Ursha explained: these older children were orphans who had been with the Missionaries of Charity since they were babies and had grown up either in Prem Dan or in one of the other Missionaries of Charity centers.

Suddenly we heard a commotion; one of the novices came running in. "Sister. Sister, please come quickly!"

We followed the novice and rushed back to the women's ward where a crowd was gathered around a female bundle groaning on the floor. Sister Ursha quelled the excited talking and was able to determine that the woman lived on the streets and had no family. She had been cooking a few days before, and her nylon sari had caught fire, ignited, and burned so fast it simply melted and stuck to her body.

The street people had taken her to a local hospital where, because she had no money, she was refused treatment, so she had been left on the street to die. The poor creature had dragged herself to the railroad tracks, possibly intending to throw herself under a train, but was eventually found and brought to Prem Dan. I did not understand why she wasn't raving from the pain.

Sister Ursha thanked the group for bringing her in and cleared the area. Then she turned to me, and believing I was a seasoned volunteer, she said she had an important appointment to collect a food donation for Prem Dan, and would I please take care of this case? I protested she had made a mistake; I didn't know what to do.

"Don't worry," she responded in a matter-of-fact way, "God knows what to do." And like the White Rabbit, she hurried off, leaving me open-mouthed in disbelief.

I stared at the pitiful creature. I had no idea where to start. I was not a doctor, nor did I even have any medical knowledge. Anybody could see this was a severe case needing expert attention and special medicines; nothing like that was here. I was frightened. I wanted to run away but I couldn't. My mind started racing. What could I do? I was only visiting. It was unfair to expect me to attend to something as major as this; someone else should do it. What if I did something wrong? What if she died? But I realized that here everyone had a task to do, and this one had fallen to me.

"Don't worry, God knows what to do," Sister Ursha had just said. Sending a plea heavenward, I hunched over the burned body and stroked the woman's face. "Dear God, if this woman is to live, then I'm willing to be your instrument. Please show me exactly what you want me to do. If she is to die, please take her fast; she's in such agony."

New York City, 1976. Ellen was my friend and mentor. We were celebrating her birthday at Les Pleiades, a favorite restaurant near Sotheby's. We were talking about the spiritual life. I was expressing confusion, between mouthfuls of smoked salmon and capers. How do I get on the spiritual path? How will I know what to do next?

What was right? What sacrifices should I make? What signs should I expect? Would there be any signs? And on and on. Ellen, chomping on a sesame stick, casually answered, "You can't possibly know what to do. Do you think Jesus knew what to do or where he was headed? All he knew to do was the next thing in front of him." With that she took another bite of her bread stick. I could not believe what I'd just heard. I leaned across the table. "What did Jesus do?"

"He did what was in front of him." She went on to talk about Jesus and his spiritual journey as though she had actually journeyed with him and as though she and he were the best of chums.

The next thing in front of him! The next thing in front of me was a burned woman. I needed help. I commandeered a young and shaky postulant, Sister Veronica. I took her by the shoulders to galvanize both of us, and together we carried the woman to the washroom, where we very gingerly cut off what remained of her clothes. Revulsion and pity welled up in me. I was overwhelmed. I had to stop and take deep breaths.

On the bare stone floor lay a human being who looked like scarcely cooked meat from the waist down. Her legs were a mass of pulpy, bleeding tissue. Maybe the two-day-old wounds were gangrenous; I didn't know. She was filthy. Part of me hoped she would die right then and there so I wouldn't have to face this hideous task. I had a thought, "What if I were to smother her with a pillow? She's so weak, she couldn't resist. She'd be dead in a few minutes and out of her agony." I forced the thought out of my mind.

It came to me that the first step was to bathe her. I scooped water with a peach preserve can out of a tin drum and poured it over her. Then Sister Veronica and I slowly washed her with disinfectant soap. Foul smells exuded from the rotting flesh around the edges of the wounds. When we had cleaned as much as we could, we doused her with a diluted disinfectant. She screamed and thrashed about but we held her down; it must have stung horribly. Then carefully, very carefully, we lifted her and carried her to the ward and laid her on a pallet.

"Oh, dear God, what is the next step?"

Then I realized the decayed and rotting flesh should be cut away. The sharpest scissors I could find was a small pair of what looked like nail scissors. I dipped them in the disinfectant, asked God to watch over us, and started cutting the burned flesh on her thigh. I gritted my teeth before making the first cut. I snipped off the obvious charred ends, and then I began cutting the deeper rot. It was like cutting into thick cloth, only this was human tissue, a living person. I sweated and stopped and started again.

For over an hour and a half, I methodically performed the grisly task. All the painkiller rations had run out; there was nothing to give her except some strong aspirin. She screamed, she shrieked, she wailed, she begged, she whimpered, she cursed, she moaned, she fainted and came to. Sister Veronica kept turning her head, and I'd hear her exhale while she gently but firmly held the woman down and wiped her brow. I felt I was committing some unspeakably cruel and demonic act. I steeled myself to block out her cries; otherwise I might have collapsed.

When I had removed as much of the dead flesh as possible, we dressed her legs and stomach with large sterile pads smeared with a special ointment for burns. We then wrapped bandages loosely around her legs and her mid-section. Now all I could do was hold her head in my lap and spoon-feed her sweet, hot tea.

I left Prem Dan spent by the ordeal. I saw nothing,

heard nothing as I made my way back to the Y. I couldn't eat and once again fell on my bed exhausted.

It was an entirely new concept to me that Jesus didn't know exactly where he was headed and that maybe he had doubts and fears like me. I had always thought Jesus knew exactly what his mission was to be—that he knew all along he was to end up on the cross. As Ellen talked, I learned about a different Jesus. I learned about a man who struggled with temptation, a man who loved life, who didn't want to die and who wanted desperately to bypass a crucifixion. A man who, when the cross was inevitably presented to him, pleaded, "Father, if thou be willing, remove this cup from me, nevertheless not my will, but thine be done." (Luke 22:42) Before meeting Ellen I had never heard anyone talk about Jesus with such ease, such familiarity, such reverence.

I woke and tried to read but couldn't; I was far too restless. I went outside and walked around the block. On the corner of Middleton and Park Road—joy of joys!—I discovered Flury's, a pastry shop and restaurant considered very grand and expensive by Calcutta standards. I was shown to a table and ordered an open, grilled-cheese-and-tomato sandwich, a pot of coffee and *three* pastries. What a relief it was to discover this place. I felt almost human again. I also felt a modicum of guilt spending so much money on pastries and a sandwich when I was witnessing so much depravation. But it didn't stop me. I was trying to forget the cutting and screaming. My innocence about human suffering was gone.

Thursday,
March 19, 1981

I returned to Prem Dan. I was afraid. I feared my hack attempts at nursing might have proved fatal, that the woman might not have lived through the night. As I made my way along the broken sidewalks I had the odd sensation of inhabiting an unfamiliar body, of simply being me—not a New Yorker, or an auctioneer, or a friend, or a daughter or even a woman. Within such a short span of time, it seemed, everything had changed for me. Nothing I had previously identified myself with seemed to have much relevance now, and to think, becoming an auctioneer had been such an enormous event in my life.

By 1976 I had been working in Sotheby's Japanese Department as a specialist and cataloger for more than five years. Preparing an auction required an almost insane capacity for attention to detail; the process could take anywhere from four months to a year. When it came time for the actual sale, however, I would have to step aside and hand the project over to an auctioneer who didn't necessarily know the first thing about Japanese art or have any personal rapport with the clients.

I became increasingly discontent with the situation. I didn't like being so involved and then not being able to complete the process; I felt like Moses must have after leading the Israelites through the desert for forty years only to be barred entry into the Promised Land. The auction was the stage where all the elements of the business came together, but since the founding of Sotheby's in London in 1744 (George Washington was twelve years old) and for the next two hundred and thirty years, not one woman had stepped into the auctioneer's rostrum. There were women on the floor of the Stock Exchange, but no woman, up to now, had wielded a gavel in the major league of fine art auctions on Madison Avenue.

I was frustrated. I wanted to be involved with the end of the process as well as the beginning. I wanted to be an auctioneer. I decided to talk to John Marion, then President of Sotheby's. It was a bold undertaking. I prepared a long and eloquent speech to deliver to him but had little hope. "No, absolutely not," I was sure would be his immediate response. So I prepared an equally long and eloquent retort to his rejection. Mindful of John's conservative leanings, I dressed with care: a tailored suit, a white silk blouse and the perfect, waspy, pale pink lipstick. I set out for Executive Row on the second floor. With a mixture of pity and amusement, my colleagues watched me enter the elevator, quite expecting me to return toute de suite, *shamefaced and humbled.*

With a feeling of daring, I knocked on the door to the inner sanctum a little too loudly and entered. John Marion sat behind a solid, dark-brown, highly-polished desk, cluttered with the usual desk paraphernalia: pens in holders, objects imprisoned in plastic, paperweights, paper clips, photographs of family members and files, files, files. There were files everywhere: files on the desk, files on the cabinet beside the desk, files on the floor, files on the sofa, files on the window sills, stack upon stack of files. I removed a pile from an upright chair opposite him and sat down. Fearing my voice might quaver, I forgot the usual social preliminaries and launched right in, "John, I'd like to be an auctioneer."

Before I could go on with my rehearsed speech, he leaned back in his chair, his fingertips together, supporting his nose, and said, "Lorna, I think that's a great idea."

I was dumbstruck. My well-prepared speech flew out through the window. I sat there staring, jaw flapping. In a light and good-humored manner, he told me to apply for a license immediately. He would train me. And that was that. Dazed, I got up from the chair, thanked him and stumbled out of the room.

Once outside, I leaned against the nearest wall and took a few deep breaths. I was to be an auctioneer! It was so simple. I flew back to the fourth floor, scarcely noticing the astonished faces of those who had pitied me just a few moments before. I sat at my desk, oblivious. My head filled with white noise. The telephone rang several times. I answered mechanically. I was going to be an auctioneer!

Producing an auction is tantamount to staging a mini-Broadway show. The auctioneer, playing a lead role, can make or break a sale; admittedly not even the greatest auctioneer can summon high prices for junk, but a poor auctioneer can conjure a dead atmosphere making a potentially interesting auction boring and lifeless and end up playing to a room of dozing bidders.

John schooled me—actually it was more like passing on a tradition. In fine art auctions it is not so much a matter of being able to roll figures off one's tongue (a factor not to be dismissed, however) as it is a matter of presence and poise. John gave me practical suggestions: study well the auctioneer's catalog before the sale; hold the gavel in one hand, the pen in the other and for God's sake DON'T switch them. Stand or sit straight with shoulders back; breathe from the abdomen. Start each lot at a fast pace. Increase the increments sensibly; keep the pace of the sale lively; reach the top price as quickly as possible; allow time at the end for that one extra bid before bringing the gavel down. I practiced John's suggestions until they became second nature. I spent hours studying old auctioneers' catalogs—standing in front of the mirror checking my posture, observing my gestures and practicing the increment increases so they rippled easily off my tongue. On weekends in the country I practiced selling to the cows in the fields, ducks on the lake. After months of preparation I was ready.

My inaugural auction took place on April 21, 1976. I had cataloged every one of the lacquer pieces and knew the sale intimately. Starting promptly at 2 pm, I waited beside the rostrum for a colleague to complete his section. I had a bad case of stage fright; actually it felt more like abject terror. It crept over me: my stomach tightened into a pebble; my mouth went dry and I wanted to bolt. I could not imagine for the life of me why I was putting myself through this agony. In my mind I saw myself haring down Madison Avenue away from Sotheby's, but somehow my feet stayed planted where they were, and while I was trying to recall why I had wanted to be an auctioneer in the first place, I heard.

"And now ladies and gentlemen, we begin the lacquer section. Miss Kelly will be your auctioneer."

He stepped out of the rostrum, wished me luck, and I stepped into his place. I closed the little door behind me, adjusted the microphone, took a deep breath and looked up to see the faces of my first audience. It was one thing to sell to munching cows and quite another to have real live people sitting in front of me ready to spend real money. I thought my heart would leap out of my rib cage, but then I heard my own calm voice say, "Ladies and gentlemen, the lacquer section begins with lot number one hundred and thirty eight, a lacquer inro *by Kagikawa, and we'll start the bidding at fifteen hundred dollars. . . ."*

I sold my first lot, and I can't remember much of what happened after that. I went on automatic—going on to sell the next lot, then the next. By the time I had sold six items, I was into the swing of it. I forgot my fear and concentrated on the sale. Rita Reif of the **New York Times** *was there. Rita who had always wanted to see a woman in the rostrum on Madison Avenue, said that if it happened, she would write a piece—so she was there recording the event. No one else knew or cared about my "debut."*

I brought the gavel down on the last lot. Very quickly it seemed it was over. The room emptied. I didn't leave straight away but stayed in the rostrum for a few moments trying to take in what had just happened, and I knew I was exactly where I was meant to be all along. I knew from that moment auctioning was in my blood. I loved what had just happened; I loved being at the center of it all, the hub of the business. I felt powerful. I liked the feeling: it was intoxicating—all eyes fixed upon me, the control of the room, the excitement, the sense of being on stage. I yearned for more glory.

My feeling of triumph was short-lived. Fast on its heels, hurtling out of the abyss, came a sudden terrible sense of deflation and emptiness—feelings that were not unfamiliar to me—a malicious thrust from the dagger of alcoholism. All the old feelings of worthlessness and inadequacy returned. Why was it that these extremes always seemed to travel hand-in-glove? I felt a black hole inside, crushing and swallowing my spirit. I walked home, fell on my bed exhausted, cried, and went to sleep. It was five-thirty in the afternoon.

When I awoke the next morning, I still felt some of the upheaval of the previous day, but it was soon diminished by the thrilling realization that I was now an auctioneer. If I doubted for a second that it had really happened, all I had to do was read the **New York Times**, which had my picture emblazoned across the front page of the second section. It was true: I was now an auctioneer at Sotheby's. I had crossed over. Thank God I hadn't bolted down Madison Avenue just before the miracle.

I walked to work down Fifth Avenue that glorious April morning, more of a bounce in my step than usual. Spring was in full swing. Central Park seemed to be sharing my enthusiasm—everything abloom and shimmering, everything new and different. Especially me. This morning an auctioneer was walking down Fifth Avenue!

At work my phone was ringing. Friends and clients were congratulating me, and the office was a profusion of flowers and telegrams. I was a star. Newspapers all over America syndicated the

New York Times article. I knew not a soul in Kansas City, and yet a headline in the Kansas City Star read, LORNA KELLY BIDDING FOR THE BIG TIME, all quite heady stuff. The feelings of worthlessness and inadequacy from the previous day went away and hid.

I was on my way to Prem Dan. I stopped at Park Circus just before the climb up the hill and purchased two small oranges from a man sitting crossed-legged on the curb. He had skillfully arranged the fruit in a circular pyramid in the basket. I gave him the four rupees he asked for; I knew it was double the regular price, but I didn't have the heart to haggle.

I was filled with relief to find the burned woman still alive, but the smell coming from her cot was absolutely putrid. The wounds at the top of her legs were smeared with her excrement and menstrual blood. In an instant my compassion and relief evaporated. I found myself hollering and screaming, "Are you crazy? Why in hell's name didn't you ask for a pan? You're destroying all my work! Lying in filth like that will infect those wounds so badly they'll never heal!"

Two novices came hurrying toward me, their faces fearful or concerned—I wasn't sure which. I caught myself. What on earth was I doing shouting at this poor, half-dead wretch, and what was I talking about, *my* work? It was all *God's* work. Fortunately, the woman couldn't understand a word I was screaming. But there was no mistaking my anger. In seconds it dissolved into overwhelming remorse. I felt ashamed. Oh God, why couldn't I control myself? I wished I were nicer, more loving. But now was no time for remorse. All the dressings had to come off, the tops of her legs had to be disinfected again, and new bandages applied.

The stench was so revolting Sister Veronica and I wore

masks. We removed the dressings. Her legs did not look any better. Mercifully, they didn't look any worse either. More of the dead flesh had to be cut away. It took time, painstaking time, to clean and redress the wounds. We carefully went through the same procedure: washing, cutting, applying the ointment, then dressing the wounds. I thought she deserved better. She was on straw pallet covered with a sheet that looked like a tablecloth with an art auctioneer to help her. But who was I to judge? The two of us had been brought together under these bizarre circumstances. She had been given to me to care for. We would never be friends; she would never come to my house for dinner; we'd never go shopping together, catch a movie, or talk on the telephone, but she would always be precious and dear to me.

When Sister Veronica and I had finished dressing her wounds, I cleaned out her ears and cut her fingernails; they were caked with filth. She seemed to like the attention. I liked the grooming and decided there and then to make the grooming a part of my service in Calcutta. I thought about how Mother Teresa served. I wondered about the woman whose work I'd come to see. I knew Mother Teresa was not a social worker; nor was her mission to run a hospital or a hospice or an orphanage; it was to serve her God. I was even more anxious to meet her.

It was the feast day of Saint Joseph; Mass was being offered in the Prem Dan chapel for the children and for those patients who could walk, crawl or shuffle there. Lying in the hallway, outside the entrance to the chapel, was a body, a dead body wrapped in a sheet—lying there, waiting for the van to come and pick it up. Curious, I lifted the flap covering the face and saw an emaciated man, probably fifty, although he could have been much younger. Who was he? Where was his family? Would his death be acknowledged by anyone who knew him, or was he was just another leaf falling in a great forest? What struck me most was the lack of diffidence with which the cadaver was treated. The children just stepped over it as though it were a log lying in the way. They probably saw dead bodies there most mornings. The tiny chapel filled up very quickly, so many of us were forced to sit in the hallway outside the open door, and to my astonishment, some of the children were actually leaning against our dead companion. It was all rather friendly; even though dead, he was included and accepted—he was still a part of life.

I had gone to view my father several times in his coffin at the funeral home. Though lifeless, he looked as he always had: his gentle face at peace, his chin a little blue where the beard continued its growth, his moustache cut crookedly, and those fine hands resting on his chest. I regretted I hadn't known him better. When I was young, he was strict and domineering, but later I knew those qualities were born out of fear. He was always worried about something—not being able to make ends meet, bringing us up right, his job. My father should never have been a policeman. He ought to have been in a gentler profession. He was sensitive and sociable and might have done well in a profession where he could charm rather than correct people. As a young man looking for a job during the Depression, however, he considered himself fortunate to have secured a position when so many were out of work. When I became an adult, my father treated me like an adult. He enjoyed my company and was proud of me. I think he was relieved to be done with raising me.

Mass over, the authorities came to remove our dead friend.

Prem Dan was not a traditional hospital; it was more of a community. The main section housed the patients in need of medical attention; there were other sections for the children, for the mentally ill, for orphans and for young girls. Most of the girls at Prem Dan had known no other home than this. When they reached marriageable age, about sixteen or seventeen, the sisters performed the duty of matchmaker.

In India an arranged marriage is the rule not the exception. In fact, I never met a husband or wife whose marriage had *not* been arranged. The best newspapers in Calcutta were chock-a-block with advertisements placed by parents offering their daughters in marriage and by men advertising themselves for suitable wives. Education, family disposition and, most important, dowry, were the selling factors for prospective brides. Beauty of face or form did not even enter the deal. A girl could be as plain as a pikestaff, but a substantial dowry made her Helen of Troy. Usually a betrothed couple did not talk to each other, much less find themselves left alone, before the wedding. Families often haggled over the dowry right up until the ceremony. After the wedding, a girl left her home to live with her new in-laws. There she was required to be subservient to her husband's mother.

Recently, there had been a terrible rash of bride burnings—situations where a husband or in-laws, finding that the dowry was insufficient or that a richer girl was available, killed the wife, usually by setting her on fire and claiming her sari had caught alight while she was boiling milk for tea. Feminists all over India were up in arms about this outbreak. In one court case it came to light that a young bride had been murdered in this shocking manner because she had not brought a transistor radio as part of her dowry. Of course, not all arranged marriages were intolerable for the woman or ended tragically; many were loving and successful. I often mused that had I let my father pick my husband, he would have made a far better choice for me than I made for myself.

From a corner of the women's ward, from behind some stacked tables, I could hear a plaintive, reedy voice chanting the same song over and over. This someone turned out to be a tiny old woman huddled in the dark. She must have been a thousand years old. Sitting on her haunches, rocking back and forth to the rhythm of her chant, she was so dusty and sparrow-like, it was quite difficult to see her there in the shadows. Apparently she had been at Prem Dan for a long time and spent a good portion of her day in that corner. She was probably chanting something she learned when she was a little girl, a beloved song that in her last days gave her great comfort. She was only one of many old women like her.

Before I went to Prem Dan, I had been told about Baloo, the "bear woman," and was curious to see her. Baloo, so the story goes, was found in the jungles of northern India. It was difficult to determine her age, but without a doubt, she had grown up wild. When first brought to the sisters over twenty years ago, she couldn't walk upright and shunted about like a bear. Whether she was actually raised by bears I'm not sure, but she certainly had not been around many humans in her formative years.

When I first saw Baloo, she was quite a sight, a squat bear-person shambling around the compound, arms and jaw thrust forward, torso incongruously clad in a gaily patterned sari. She looked like a bear. Her feet were as flat as could be, and her toes had a prehensile look about them. She was no more than four feet tall; her back was bent, and her little eyes peered out from beneath a heavy overhanging brow. Her face with its flattened features had a definite feral look. She had learned a few words of Bengali and English, but mostly she grunted. Nevertheless, the sisters were very proud she had learned so much: she had learned to relieve herself in one particular place, to make her bed, to dress herself and to keep her little area tidy.

Baloo had a friend—Angela. Angela was as mad as a hatter and looked it. She was quite the opposite of Baloo— tall, slim, with an elegant bearing. She looked strangely like an ostrich: enormous, dark circular eyes set in a tiny, round head, crowned with tufty wisps of hair, perched atop a very long neck. She often stood perfectly still, moving only her head slowly, from side to side. Baloo was fiercely protective of her weird friend, who, incidentally, never spoke a word, not one syllable. Maybe Baloo instinctively sensed in her silent companion something damaged—something that needed cherishing. I was sure if one went too near Angela or did something Baloo didn't like, Baloo would show her teeth and growl, perhaps even attack and bite if pushed too far. They were an oddly adorable couple; they had found companionship and were happy together.

Movies, magazines and my own limited experience of the world had shaped my ideas of love. I believed, like so many girls, I would one day meet Prince Charming, marry, have children, etc., etc., etc. The first time I met John Kelly, I flipped. We had a romantic courtship. Kelly was six years older than I and seemed sophisticated in an artistic sort of way; he even looked like a blond Vincent Van Gough. He was quiet, gentle and soft-spoken; in fact, in the beginning, I was constantly having to ask him to speak louder. He was charming. He was always at ease; "laid back" was the term his friends used to describe him. We married in 1966. We divorced in 1976. Not one of my dreams was realized. Our lives together simply, sadly, disintegrated. Alcohol and alcoholism ruled us.

When the marriage was over and I had moved to my own

apartment, I found myself drinking alone, something I hadn't done before. I told myself it was all right; I worked hard and deserved to come home and relax with a drink or two. Wouldn't anyone do the same in my situation? Some evenings I couldn't be bothered to get undressed and fell asleep in my clothes with a blanket pulled over me. I never felt more alone.

At Kalighat in the afternoon, I held an old woman in my arms as she drew her last breath. There was a slight shudder as her soul departed her body, and that was that. I didn't know her name; I knew nothing about her; I wondered why it was that we should be together at this momentous time in her life. I wondered what it all meant, or if it meant anything at all. I helped wrap her in a sheet and, with another volunteer, carried her to the tiled room. There were no relatives to inform, no children to mourn her death— another leaf dropping in the forest.

My own father had died unexpectedly. It happened in May, 1977, while he and my mother were touring Wales. In his last letter to me, he wrote how much he was looking forward to their holiday and to my visit home the following month. There was a postscript wishing me luck with my auction at the Plaza Hotel—the dreaded Plaza. I'd never be able to amuse him with the story of that evening's fiasco.

I had arranged a trip to Israel in three weeks time and had planned to break the journey in London to visit my parents, but I had a nagging sense things were just not going to work out quite the way I'd planned. I shared my premonitions with friends, but it didn't take away the dull, unexplainable ache in my heart. My parents embarked on their trip to Wales on a Saturday morning in mid-May. The day before they left, I had wanted so much to call and wish them a pleasant holiday, but by the time I had a free moment, it was too late to call England, so I sat at my desk and replied to my father's letter instead.

Monday morning in the office, I got a call from my sister Helen to say that father had suffered a stroke in Llandudno and that he'd been rushed to the local hospital. The doctors didn't think it serious and felt confident he would pull through. I knew it was the end, but neither my heart nor my head would handle it. I allowed a soothing denial to set in, telling myself he'd had a heart attack once before and had recovered, so I need not rush home. The small child inside me was saying, "If you don't go, he'll be all right."

The next morning was a glorious, spring morning. My sister called again. It was all over.

The whole world suddenly looked sharp—everything in keen focus. It's curious how death seems to heighten the senses. I had no immediate feeling of sadness; everything appeared to be just as it should be, in Divine Right Order.

I called the travel agent, booked a flight and went home to pack. In the late afternoon I took a bus to the airport and boarded the plane to Manchester. As the plane sat on the runway, I looked out the window at a large, orange sun setting in the west and felt a profound peace. It was as though my father were with me. I had the sense that, having shed his body, he had now assumed his true nature. He might have died but he hadn't gone away, and strangely, now that time and distance no longer separated us, I felt he was more accessible to me. I had a new sense of the word "remains," and felt I was going home only as a sign of respect for his earthly sojourn and to dispose of the housing he had cast off.

On arrival at the Manchester airport I was met by my brother and sister, and we drove to Wales. At the hotel in Llandudno my grieving mother greeted me, "Oh Lorna, your father was so proud of you."

During the next few days the four of us spent many hours together sharing memories of Father. Old images tumbled out of the long-buried past and now were vivid: I was five years old, playing in the back garden, when he came out of the house dressed in his uniform with its silver buttons and the distinctive tall helmet of the English bobby. "Daddy, why do you have to go to work?" I asked.

"To keep you and your mother in luxury," was his jolly reply as he pushed off on his battered orange bicycle.

We had my father cremated in Llandudno and carried his ashes back to London for a memorial service. When we arrived at my parents' house, I opened the front door, and on the mat was the letter I had written him.

Before I left New York a friend had given me the name and address of June Pathickaden in Calcutta. My friend had met June at a party in New York and asked if I would look her up. Mrs. Moffat, from the Y, gave me directions, and after the evening meal, I made my way to the address on Elliot Road. To have found the correct location in the maze of confusing streets was, I thought, quite an accomplishment.

June rented rooms in a flat on the second floor of what had once been an elegant mansion. Three boys in the courtyard were playing cricket with a stick for a bat and a popped tennis ball; they stopped and stared at me as I ascended the wooden flight of stairs on the outside of the house. The door to the flat was slightly ajar. There was no bell or doorknocker, so I rapped on the frame. A light, English voice trilled, "Come in, come in."

I entered a dingy, spacious room with an overstuffed sofa and a couple of chairs. A coffee table covered with newspapers was listing to one side in front of the sofa, one leg shorter than its mates. A dining room set straight out of my parents' home was in the rear of the room. June emerged from behind a curtain to the left of me. She was Anglo-Indian, so she informed me immediately. She was an attractive vivacious woman in her early fifties, with olive skin, dark short hair, high cheekbones and bright eyes. She had a wonderful mannered, 1930's British accent and used phrases I hadn't heard since my school days.

"Apologies, apologies, you'll have to excuse me in this old rig-out." She was wearing an ancient nylon nightdress pinned at the neck with a safety pin and a Miraculous Medal. But she displayed a certain flair even in her "old rig-out." I introduced myself, and she behaved as though we'd known each other for years, revealing intimate information about herself and asking what I thought to be some rather bold questions about me and my family background. But she hardly waited for an answer before skipping on to the next question or topic. It did not take long to discover she was a marathon talker and getting a word in edgeways was nigh impossible. Strangely enough, I wasn't bothered. She was articulate and highly entertaining. Her *ayah* made tea and we sat and chatted or, more accurately, she chatted and I listened. Two hours later, I left, promising to return.

Friday,
March 20, 1981

I walked to Prem Dan by myself. I had saved my banana and slices of toast from breakfast and had given them to Blondine's Madonna-like girl I'd seen a few days before. I was rewarded with that same beatific smile. How could she be so radiant under such appalling conditions?

As I neared Prem Dan, I could see there was a commotion on the bridge. People were leaning over the parapet talking excitedly and pointing towards the railway line. I learned that just a few minutes before, a young woman had leapt off the bridge into the path of an oncoming train. She was killed outright. Family members in the crowd were distraught and wailing; most of the onlookers, however, appeared curious but at the same time indifferent, almost nonchalant. Children, in their usual state of nakedness, played in the gutter and on the sidewalk, oblivious to the tragedy that had just occurred.

From what I could make out, the dead woman's husband had beaten her and thrown her out after he had learned she had gone to the movies with a male friend—not a lover, just a family friend. For a poor Indian woman to be thrown out by her husband is a death sentence; rarely can she return to her own family. Her lack of education prevents her from seeking the scanty legal help available; her community confirms she has no redress, leaving her to choose prostitution or suicide.

The approach to Prem Dan was lined on both sides of the road with shanties. The unfortunate woman had belonged to this community of squalid hovels covered with sacking and plastic sheets, blackened with soot, crammed together with no privacy, no real protection (except from the sun's glare), no running water. Going to the movies was probably the highlight in her dreary life.

As waves erase footprints on a beach, life quickly returned to normal. People started to move away and get on with their own business. With the chatter of the onlookers and the lamenting of family and friends still in my ears, I left the bridge and entered Prem Dan.

I was glad to plunge into the day's work and put aside what had just happened. I went straight to the burned woman's cot. Sister Veronica was waiting for me. We had become friends. She was a shy, serious young woman who had been with the Missionaries of Charity for almost a year and confided to me that although she missed her family from the south of India, she was "so happy to be with Jesus." She translated for me, not that there was much translating to do since the patient hardly spoke.

The wounds were pretty much the same as yesterday, but no cutting of flesh was needed. We started working. It took us time to cut away the bandages, clean the area of pus, apply the ointment and rewrap her legs and stomach. I didn't hold out much hope of their healing; they were in an awful state. The woman was still in dreadful pain, but her face was not quite so wracked. She was alert and watchful. As I left her, I could feel her eyes following me.

The Missionaries of Charity employed about thirty women at Prem Dan—paid in grain and oil—to do various chores: laundry, cooking, taking care of the children, and generally assisting the sisters. One woman had no legs and moved about on a small wooden board mounted on casters.

Her job was to administer medicine, when available, to the patients. She knew exactly who got what and rolled around the ward between the cots chatty and happy, proud of her work and responsibility. She would give the shot or pill and then record who had received what in a ledger. I found it remarkable. A person with such a handicap would surely not be allowed to scoot around the wards of an American hospital on a little wooden trolley, and yet no hospital could have on its staff a more dedicated or efficient worker.

I noticed all the foodstuffs at Prem Dan were in sacks and cans marked "A Gift from the People of the United States of America."

Today I was able to spend time with some of the other women patients. Most were very old, cast out by husbands and circumstances years before; many were mentally ill— all had their hair cropped. They seemed happy enough, huddled together in groups chatting or arguing. More than likely they would remain at Prem Dan until they died. There was a roly-poly woman named Monica. She was mentally retarded, had slightly deformed feet and sat on her bed Buddha-like, her short, fat legs crossed and her back held perfectly straight. She had a pile of multi-colored beads in her lap and compulsively strung, unstrung and restrung them in different patterns, over and over. I never heard her talk and rarely saw her pay attention to anyone or anything going on around her, so concentrated was she on her task. Occasionally we were treated to her smile; it would spread across her child-like face and light up the bleak dormitory.

There were other women who were not old or mentally ill; they were mostly recovering from TB. They were friendly and companionable in an effortless, simple manner, and I enjoyed their company. They were fascinated with a packet of tissue I had with me. That one tissue popped out right after the other, and that I had something so clean and soft to blow my nose on and then discard, appeared to them to be the absolute height of luxury. I let them have the packet but said that in return they had to show me how to wear a sari. They took on the project with great delight and seriousness, but very quickly we were all in stitches.

Each day delivered up more victims of the cruel streets. Each day I witnessed anew countless sights of suffering. I had no idea the human body could endure so much, be so emaciated, diseased, crippled, so covered with sores and still not die. I saw children horribly deformed, some purposely mutilated so they could beg. No matter how severe the deformities and amputations, hardly any wheelchairs, crutches, or prostheses of the type common in the West were in evidence. The lame used crude homemade crutches or dragged themselves along the ground.

A woman no more than twenty-five, but who looked much older, was "walking" on her knees; her lower legs were shriveled and horribly maimed. There was no padding or cushion between her flesh and the rough ground. Her daughter, a seven-year old, was also a victim, permanently enslaved to her crippled mother. I wondered how this woman, forced onto all fours to get about, had become pregnant in the first place. She had probably been raped or at least taken advantage of—she was certainly helpless.

I spent the afternoon at Kalighat clipping nails and cleaning ears. When I arrived at the Mother House in the evening for Adoration, there was a lot of chatter and excitement; Mother Teresa was due home sometime the next day. It seemed amazing that five days had already passed since I arrived in India, and I couldn't help feeling excited, too—excited at the prospect of finally meeting the woman whose life had already had a profound effect on mine.

After dinner I went to visit June Pathickaden again. I hoped she'd be at home. There was no way to telephone beforehand, since a telephone was a luxury found in very few homes in Calcutta; those that did exist were enormous, clunky and weighed a ton—if one were to lift the receiver too swiftly to one's ear, there was the real possibility of knocking oneself unconscious. And since Calcutta was subject to almost daily power outages, telephones, like most other electrical appliances, seldom worked.

The flat where June lived actually belonged to Mrs. Bateman, a former headmistress who now tutored in English. When I arrived, Mrs. Bateman was sitting at the dining room table in the rear of the flat with one of her pupils, a frightened-looking lad in a disheveled school uniform—maroon and silver-striped tie around his neck like a hangman's noose, short grey pants and a once-white shirt. He had a mop of blue/black hair, and his feet were twisting with anxiety under the table. He was having some difficulty with prepositions, and every time he made a mistake, Mrs. Bateman boxed him soundly around his ears. Whenever we heard a slap, we'd stop talking, and June would raise her eyes heavenward and shake her head; she obviously disapproved of Mrs. Bateman's techniques. At last the lesson was over; I heard a "Thank you, madam," and the small boy, full of shame, scurried past us and out the door. His ears were quite red despite his dark complexion.

Mrs. Bateman joined us; she, too, was an Anglo-Indian—a tall, big-boned, stately looking woman in her mid-sixties. She was wearing a floral frock, English tea-party, circa 1955. She was quite charming, but I found myself a little wary of her; I couldn't quite erase the image of her boxing the boy's ears just moments earlier.

This evening June was her usual animated self, talking non-stop, never quite finishing one story before weaving into another. It took her ages to get to the point, normally the sort of thing that drove me up the wall, but I was quite happy to relax and listen. June was good-natured and generous; I liked her company and her never-ending wealth of tales, and being with her felt comfortably like England.

Saturday,
March 21, 1981

For some reason, this morning I decided to sit in a different place in the chapel facing one end of the room with the altar on my right. I was absorbed in prayer for a while, but when I looked up, I saw an older nun whom I hadn't seen before. I was startled to realize it was Mother Teresa. She was sitting right in front of me, her back to the wall, facing the altar, in the same spot where I had sat every other morning! I had no idea it was her place, and no one had ever asked me to move. She was sitting as the Missionaries of Charity usually sit, on the floor with her legs curled to one side. Her head was lowered almost to her chest in deep prayer. After being at Mass with Mother countless times, I came to realize she was in fact often taking a much-needed nap—cradled in the arms of God.

Mother Teresa was the first in the chapel, and as I, too, happened to arrive earlier than usual, I was able to be with her in prayerful silence for a few minutes before the others streamed in. By 5 am the chapel was tightly packed with sisters for morning prayers, and just before Mass at 6:30 am, some locals and a few volunteers joined the congregation.

Mother Teresa was first in line to receive Communion. By her demeanor I felt I was watching a woman engaged in the one thing in the world she lived for—being with her beloved. Once she had received Communion, she assisted the priest by taking a chalice to the other end of the chapel to distribute the body of Christ. She placed a host on each and every tongue, sharing her "heart-of-hearts" lovingly with her sisters. Then she replaced the chalice on the altar and returned to her place. No sooner had she settled down, eyes closed, than some lunatic Japanese fellow with cameras slung all over his body like a Hollywood Mexican bandit, all but sat in Mother's lap, snapping and clicking away. At one point he was lying down beside her and aiming the camera up her nostrils. She didn't move a muscle. I wondered if she was offering up this annoyance to God. Sister Frederick finally shooed him away.

Mass over, Mother Teresa stood barefoot on the balcony outside the chapel to greet visitors—people like me, who had come to Calcutta because they were curious about her work and eager to meet her. I took note of her bearing, frail yet unshakable. She was slightly stooped and looked up from under her brows. She wore her habit shorter than the others, revealing thick ankles and solid feet. Some of her toes were bent, curled one over the other. They were feet made tough by sandals' traversing the slums and mean streets of the world, doing God's work. Her stalwart peasant looks belied her background, which originated in the Albanian, educated middle-class.

At the age of twelve, Agnes Gonxha Bojaxhiu knew she wanted to be a nun and a missionary. At the age of eighteen, she left her home in Skopje, Albania, and journeyed to Ireland to join the Loretto Sisters. There she went through her novitiate and took the name Teresa after Saint Teresa of Lisieux. In 1928 she made the seven-week sea voyage to Calcutta to enter the Loretto convent there and teach. In 1946 she was on a train to Darjeeling to make her annual retreat, when, as she puts it, she received "a call within a call." She felt

God was asking her to leave the security of the Loretto convent to go out onto the streets and serve Him in the slums with the poorest of the poor. In 1948 she took off the veil and the habit she had worn for so long and donned the cheapest of white cotton saris (worn only by the lowliest Indian women) over her Loretto nightshirt. She left the sisters of Loretto, a community she loved, a home she'd known for twenty years, to step into the unknown.

I scrutinized her face. It was a face furrowed with deep wrinkles, a face that had never seen creams or moisturizers. Her expression was one of tranquil alertness. I felt sure this old lady missed very little. I towered over her. When it came my turn to meet her, I introduced myself and we had a polite chat. She spoke perfect English with an interesting European/Indian accent. She was very nice. She asked me where I was from and how long I would be in Calcutta—general questions. I answered simply. I found myself a little in awe of her. I wanted to stay in her company longer, but there were others waiting to talk to her. Reluctantly I moved on.

So I had met the renowned Mother Teresa whom the sisters simply referred to as Mother. A few minutes and it was all over. I wondered if I would see her again. When I had first made my booking for India, I had told myself it wasn't important whether I met her or not. But now I *had* met her and felt something in her presence; I had a strange longing to see her again. I suppose I should have been grateful to have had the privilege of shaking her hand and spending a few minutes in her company. "Besides," I asked myself, "Had I not come to Calcutta mainly to see the work and not the woman?" Jesus' words had inspired me: "Believe me, if not for me, for the work's sake." (John 14:11) Chastened I walked to Prem Dan, but my head still buzzed with the encounter.

The burned woman's wounds had moisture in them, the beginning of healing. I could hardly believe it. She was a long way from being out of the woods, but there was a good chance she wouldn't lose her legs. The speed of the healing had the unmistakable hallmark of a Higher Power's handiwork. How could those dreadful wounds have started to heal otherwise?

I allowed myself to get closer to the woman. I had had to detach myself in order to serve her and myself. Now I sat on a low stool beside her, talking to her and holding her hand. With Sister Veronica acting as interpreter, I learned her name was Meeta and that she came from a small village outside Calcutta. She had been married, but her husband had thrown her out. I wondered if, in fact, she was a victim of bride-burning. Was she too ashamed to admit it? Was she ashamed because she hadn't measured up to her husband's expectations?

This was all conjecture on my part. I had no idea what the true story was. My thoughts were probably colored by the suicide on the bridge the other morning. She was not a pretty woman. Her features were rather coarse and toughened, I'm sure, by the pain she was now suffering. She was penniless, had no home, no family, and she would now have a badly scarred body. I wondered what she would do. I took a measure of comfort in thinking God had saved her life for a reason.

In the afternoon I walked the short distance from the Mother House to Shishu Bhavan, the home for very young orphans. Shishu Bhavan was light and airy, crammed with cots and filled with babies, some asleep, some wailing, some just in their cribs looking around, some being fed. There was a whole row of them sitting on potties. All the babies had been found abandoned on the streets or in garbage dumps—

or had been deposited on the doorsteps of the Missionaries of Charity—or had been brought in by the police or other city agencies. Most of them were adopted by Indian couples, but some went to foreign lands.

While I was there, several delighted couples from Europe and Australia came to collect their new son or daughter. It was moving to witness children being taken from the sisters to be given to their new parents. There was much shrieking and wailing as little arms reached back to the only mothers they had known. The change took only a minute or two but would transform their lives forever. Later in the afternoon, I returned to Kalighat, to the house of the dying. The beginning of life, the end of life.

Mother Teresa was at Adoration in the afternoon. We didn't talk, but I felt it a great privilege to be with her during prayers. When it was time for the exposition of the Blessed Sacrament, she approached the tabernacle, sank to her knees and bowed her forehead to the floor; then she stood again and with care, love and concentration, opened the tiny door, removed the host and placed it in the monstrance. Again she was on her knees bowing, forehead to the floor, wholly absorbed. She was unashamedly in love. Undiluted passion exuded from this seventy-one-year-old virgin. She was pure, consecrated, spoken for. It was awesome to witness. I felt caught up in the power of a mystical love beyond my understanding.

Sunday,
March 22, 1981

I was late this morning so, for the first time, I hailed a rickshaw and was surprised, even though we traversed some pretty bumpy roads, at how fast we traveled.

When I first arrived in Calcutta, I swore I'd never hire a rickshaw. I told myself I was quite capable of walking or taking a regular taxi and that I was not about to promote the practice of paying a human to be a beast of burden. The sight of men pulling rickshaws disturbed me. The drivers led a hard and usually brief life—not that others in Calcutta had it easy—but the rickshaw drivers were so visible. They were all skinny; their narrow rib cages revealed every bone, their limbs straining every sinew as they ran through the streets, hitched between the shafts of their ricks. They were remarkably adept at maneuvering their loads in and out of the spaces on jammed thoroughfares all the while banging a small brass bell against one of the shafts. Most drivers ran barefoot, wearing just a *longhi* and maybe a T-shirt. They lived on the streets and, not being able to abandon their ricks for fear of theft, slept under them at night. During the monsoon season rickshaws were the only vehicles that could be navigated through the flooded streets. The drivers' health suffered irreparably during this lucrative period. Often riddled with TB by the age of thirty-five, they ended up in Kalighat or Prem Dan.

Having been in Calcutta for a week, I realized my Western opinions of the system were doing nothing but depriving a man of a fare. I would better serve him by going on a diet and thereby lightening his load.

After Mass Mother Teresa again stood on the balcony and addressed the few visitors and volunteers. I felt unusually shy and contented myself with only observing her. I was still in awe of the unabashed display of love I'd witnessed the evening before at Adoration and remembered the beginning of my own love affair with Jesus.

I was scheduled to take a sale of Japanese art to Hawaii. I planned to stay on in Honolulu after the sale to relax and read about Jesus. Ellen had sparked my interest, and I wanted to know more about Him, but what to read? I trotted off to Paraclete, a Catholic bookstore on East 74th Street. Not having a clue what books to ask for and to overcome my awkwardness, I stood in the middle of the shop and asked in a rather loud, grand voice radiating in all directions, "Do you by any chance have a book about Jesus as a human being?"

A salesman approached and, perhaps sensing I was a beginner, kindly responded to my question as though it had great theological significance. He respectfully suggested I might enjoy **Christ the Lord** *by Gerard S. Sloyan. Armed with this one slim paperback, I set off on my travels.*

On a beach in Hawaii, I read my 95-cent, 195-page book about Jesus. I read it from cover to cover. When I finished, I wept. I don't quite know why I wept. Maybe I wept because I identified with Jesus' struggles and doubts. Maybe because I felt if I followed Jesus' example by surrendering my life to God, the possibilities were endless. Maybe because I had met the ultimate lover. I had discovered my pearl of great price and knew, absolutely, this gem was worth relinquishing everything I had to own it. I had always wanted a cause, something I could devote my life to, and here it was—His life. Christ's life. Mother Teresa had done precisely that in a no-frills way; she was worldly and wise, and the work I was witnessing started because of her singular devotion to Jesus. Mother Teresa continually urged us to see, as she did, Jesus in "the distressing disguise of the poor" and to offer every minute of our day as a prayer.

I had planned to go to Prem Dan with Etienne, a young French doctor, and forgot to buy yogurt. Etienne was with a group who had been in Calcutta for a while volunteering at the various Missionaries of Charity centers. He said this hands-on medical training was a fantastic opportunity he could never possibly hope to have as an intern in Paris. His thin, sensitive face reflected the zeal he had for his work as he talked about his experiences in Calcutta.

We walked along Park Street. Outside the main post office, professional writers sat cross-legged on the pavement in front of their portable desks, complete with porcelain inkwells and dip-pens. The professional writers provided an invaluable service in a city where a huge percentage of the population was illiterate. For a nominal sum they would compose and write letters or fill out documents. I never saw them idle; customers crowded around them like chicks around a mother hen and waited their turn.

As we passed one of the colonies of slums, a ragged fellow beckoned us. Etienne and I followed him down a short alley to a courtyard where a mangy brown bear was muzzled and chained. The wretched animal had a hole pierced through the top of its nose through which a tethering rope was passed. The bear was filthy, flea-bitten, half-starved and had absolutely no chance of escape or rescue. I could scarcely stand to look at the scene. The ragged fellow asked us for a few *paise* to watch the bear dance. I didn't know who was sadder, the man or the beast. We gave him some rupees but didn't wait for the performance. A sense of hopelessness overwhelmed me.

At Prem Dan, Etienne examined Meeta's wounds. Scabs were beginning to form on some of them. He was amazed she had survived such severe burns and that her legs hadn't turned gangrenous. He kept shaking his head in wonder and then showed Sister Veronica and me how to wrap the bandages properly. Meeta took my hand, pressed it against her forehead and then kissed it. It was a surprising gesture, and I felt tears flood my eyes.

When we had made her as comfortable as possible, Etienne took me to the headquarters of the Natural Family Planning program housed in a long shack just beyond the coconut-stripping yard. Sister Paulette was in charge. Etienne had heard about Sister Paulette's work and had been anxious to meet her, but every time he'd been at Prem Dan before, she'd been out. Sister Paulette was from the French island of Mauritius just off the west coast of India, and she seemed just as delighted to meet Etienne as he was finally to catch up with her. They nattered away for a while in French while I looked at the discolored charts of reproductive organs on the walls. The paperweight on her desk was a crucifix with its arms missing.

Suddenly, Sister Paulette turned to me and said, "So! Here is the Queen of Calcutta." I had no idea what she was talking about and must have looked puzzled. She probably had me mixed up with someone else. Laughing, she explained she was indeed talking about me. I had won the nickname among the sisters by my regal entrances into the Mother House so early in the mornings. She said no one else had ever come that early to join the sisters for morning prayers, and she was the one in charge of making sure a novice was at the door at that hour to let me in.

I was amazed. I didn't really think anyone had taken any notice of me; I thought they were far too engrossed with their devotions, and I certainly didn't feel particularly regal, but I had to admit it wasn't the first time I'd heard myself described this way. I was amused not only to hear her account but also to realize the sisters chatted this way among themselves and were really not so different from the rest of us. I liked this nun's openness and good humor. She talked about her work; most days she was out of Prem Dan travelling to villages, teaching women about a natural method of birth control. She invited us to join her on one of her trips, so we could see for ourselves how the program worked. We said we'd be thrilled.

It was blisteringly hot as Etienne and I walked slowly back to the Y, yet even in the worst heat, the Y was cool. Like so much of Calcutta, the Y was a leftover from the days of the British Raj. Most of the city looked as though someone had blown a whistle in 1947 and everything had stopped just where it was, except that the once grand buildings were now decaying and crumbling. The whole city had the feel of Miss Haversham's house in Dickens's *Great Expectations*—as though the clocks had been stopped.

My stomach was upset, probably because I hadn't eaten my morning yogurt, so I skipped lunch, not much of a sacrifice. Later I walked to the Mother House for Adoration and allowed myself to be lulled by the prayers. My stomach was still queasy at dinnertime. I didn't dare risk the Y cuisine. A cheese and tomato sandwich and a chocolate eclair in Flury's seemed a far better choice.

Monday,
March 23, 1981

In March, 1963, Mother Teresa, seeing that the orphan boys in her care needed male guidance and supervision, founded the Missionary Brothers of Charity. The brothers were mostly in charge of schools and centers for street boys, and they ran the leprosy clinics. One of the brothers was celebrating his feast day, so Mother left after morning prayers to join them for Mass in another part of Calcutta. I was surprised at the niggling sense of loss I felt by her absence and walked back to the Y feeling slightly dejected. I missed her morning talk. I did, however, make sure to buy yogurt.

At breakfast I was made anxious when somebody mentioned how erratic flights out of Calcutta could be—they rarely left on time and were often simply cancelled. I became agitated. Nothing worked in this city. If the powers-that-be could not even get the telephones to work, how on earth would they be able to get a huge jet off the ground? My plan was to stay in Calcutta for three weeks, and now three weeks seemed as long as the T'ang dynasty.

The prospect of staying longer than I'd planned, having my sensibilities assailed every day by the sight of hunger, pain and poverty, was too much. I had a dreadful feeling of being trapped in this awful alien place and of never being able to get out. All my efforts of living in the present evaporated, and I was wrapped up in future projections of what I'd do if my out-bound flight were delayed. After wasting half an hour on this futile exercise, Etienne and I set off for the Kidderpore district to work in the Missionaries of Charity dispensary. It was a relief to be caught up in the work; it helped dispel the anxiety. "Look upward and outward, give each moment to God." Mother's words were magically in my ears.

Outside the clinic, which was really just a shed, a crowd of women waited. Many held up their sickly children to us, pleading for help. The children for the most part were malnourished or ravaged by diseases. The pain and concern on each mother's face was heartbreaking.

Inside the clinic Etienne got to work. The children were dirty and barely covered in grimy, tattered clothes, their hair crawling with lice. The noise was deafening—each woman pushing and shoving to get her child seen next, the babies screaming, the older kids crying. It was a zoo. Many children were riddled with worms; their swollen bellies were testament to the parasites they hosted. Eye infections were all too common in a city where the polluted air was full of particles from the dung, coal fires and diesel trucks and buses. There were children with thick yellowish stuff oozing from their tightly closed eyes. Etienne tried to get one small boy to open his eyes to bathe them; but the child could not; he was probably already blind. Etienne shook his head and in a frustrated tone told the sister in charge to ask the boy's mother why she hadn't brought her son in sooner. The poor woman simply wept. Etienne realized it was pointless to berate her. The damage had been done.

Another boy was limping because of a huge boil on the heel of his foot. The sight of us terrified him, and he struggled to get away. Eventually we overpowered him by tying his hands and sitting on him. One of the volunteers, a trained nurse, swiftly lanced the boil and squeezed it, whereupon a sudden jet of green pus shot clear across the room. The boy howled and thrashed about; it was like trying to hold down a shrieking wildcat, but we kept sitting and she kept squeezing until it was completely drained. We then dressed the sore and sent the boy on his way. We were exhausted.

There followed a multitude of ailments: ear infections, sores, burns and wounds of every sort. There were children with scabies and ringworm who were manic from the itching and scratching; the filthy surroundings they lived in continually exacerbated their conditions.

I had been a sickly baby and spent my first three weeks of life in an incubator. My mother was anxious through most of her pregnancy, running back and forth to air-raid shelters with my brother clutched to her whenever the warning sirens sounded. World War II ended in Britain in 1945, two months before I was born, but the food shortages didn't end. My mother, like so many others, bore the consequences of poor nutrition during pregnancy. I developed rickets and, until the age of seven, my arms would easily come out of their sockets. I clearly remember trips to the doctor to have them excruciatingly painfully adjusted back into position.

My lungs were no less fragile. I was susceptible to colds and had violent coughing bouts that soaked me in sweat leaving me wracked and nigh dead with the effort. England, with its bone-invading dampness and lack of central heating, was not the ideal place for a sickly child. Medicine and a spoon were kept on my bedside table, but I shook too much to be able to pour the correct dose. I put the bottle directly to my lips for long swigs of the remedy. Laced with alcohol, it did the trick and soothed me until it knocked me out. Every winter was the same—the cold damp would start and so would my cough.

A nagging sense of hopelessness returned. The multitude of mothers and their sick offspring intensified my pessimism.

I hated the poverty; I saw nothing noble or redeeming about it. Nonetheless I was somehow removed from the experience, and I was aware of my detachment. I let myself observe Calcutta without allowing it to touch me too deeply. I kept saying to myself, "I'm different from these people." Was it true? Was I different? Or had I merely erected a strong barrier as a defense against so much suffering? I realized what I really felt was pity and only rarely true compassion. It was clear to me I was not on the same spiritual plane as Mother Teresa. I stayed at the dispensary until it closed at one o'clock. I was sweaty, fatigued, and irritable. Etienne and I hardly spoke as we traveled back to the Y for lunch.

No matter how late we were, our meals at the Y were put aside for us in an ancient tin cupboard with chipped paint and wire mesh doors. By the time we arrived, they were usually congealed and cold, but still the waiters presented them with great flourish, as if they were a rare delicacy. Meals, either on time or late, were served by a team of male waiters who, I judged, had been at the Y since Gunga Din and were wearing their original issue of uniforms. They were clad in the grubbiest khaki outfits and shuffled around in rubber flip-flops. To add an air of formality, each had a stained tea towel draped over one arm and performed as if he were serving a banquet at Buckingham Palace.

In India I found the speech and actions of those in service were of the highest standard, always polite and formal, even in the scruffiest milieu. All the British mannerisms had been retained despite the decline in circumstance and respectability. Now, seated in the dining room, I unleashed my irritation at the condition of my food. I sniffed and tutted, pulled faces and groaned. I did everything except tell the waiter outright that the meal was not fit for human consumption. I ate it in any case.

I left the dining room and relaxed in my room for a while; then feeling refreshed, I decided to board a mini-bus to Gol Park to visit the Ramakrishna Center, a religious cultural institute. The Center was set in landscaped grounds and was quite delightful; there were paved walks meandering between fountains and fragrant flowerbeds. A variety of different birds, besides the ever-pervasive crows, chirped and flitted about. Benches were placed under pleasant shade trees; the whole atmosphere conveyed a sense of tranquility. It was good to be in pretty surroundings, to see another side of Calcutta where people were not struggling to survive. My pessimism lifted. I felt human again.

By the time I left the Center, it was dusk; the western sky was a ruddy smudge. I felt renewed and more hopeful about staying on in Calcutta, and I had changed my mind: when I had first made plans, I had toyed with the idea of visiting other places in India, but now I wanted to stay put. I wanted to make my sojourn here a mission, not play the tourist and dash off here and there. The Taj Mahal wasn't going anywhere; I could see it some other time. What was happening right now was unique, even if it did not always feel so wonderful. By the time I arrived at the Mother House for Adoration, I felt almost exuberant.

I had seen Mother Teresa every morning, but we hadn't spoken since our first very polite meeting. This evening, before Adoration, we talked again. It didn't start well. I was standing in the courtyard about to go upstairs to the chapel when she returned to the house with some of the sisters. As she passed by, I said, "Hello, Mother." She stopped and without looking me in the eye, she took my hand and pointed at my red fingernails. "Why do you wear that stuff?"

I was taken aback by the obvious disapproval and annoyance in her voice. I didn't quite know what to say and stammered defensively, "I wear it because I think it's decorative."

Wrong answer! "You should decorate your heart," she said in the same tone. "Besides, nail polish is expensive, and it would be better if you sold what you have and gave the money to the poor."

Suddenly I was furious. I had been deluded into thinking she was a darling, little lady, all sweetness and light. Gone completely were my feelings of awe and admiration for her. How dare this midget, done up in what looked like an oversized tea towel, tell me how to dress or what to wear and what to do with my money! Who did she think she was? I know now my indignation was covering more than a little hurt pride that she didn't think me the bee's knees or recognize me as a spiritual equal.

"Selling one's cosmetics and giving the money to the poor, I seem to remember, is exactly what Judas suggested to Jesus," I fired back—a salvo of heavy sarcasm.

There, standing in the courtyard, everything stopped. Mother looked me in the eye; we held each other's gaze for a full ten seconds, stock-still and ready, two gunfighters facing each other at high noon waiting to see who would draw first. The sisters were open-mouthed.

As soon as the words had escaped my mouth, I was filled with regret and would have done *anything* to be able to take them back, but I just stood there feeling prideful, hurt and out of place. It was all over for me; I had just committed the ultimate transgression. I had been rude to Mother Teresa. Well, I might just as well crawl back to New York and die.

Then Mother laughed. It was in fact more of a chuckle; maybe she was surprised someone who looked the way I did could quote scripture. I laughed, too, more from a sense of relief and gratitude than amusement. She then drew me aside and said she noticed me in the chapel at morning prayers and meditation, and never before had one of the volunteers come that early. I was astonished. I didn't realize she knew me from a hole in the wall. She asked where I was working.

"I've been doing some service at Kalighat and some at Prem Dan. I met Sister Paulette, and this morning I worked at the dispensary at Kidderpore."

"*Acha, acha*," (good, good) she replied, "how do you like working with our poor people?"

"Well, actually, Mother, I find it difficult. I find myself impatient a lot of the time. I really dislike this quality in myself, but I'm afraid it's the truth."

"Not to worry. Keep the love of Jesus in your heart and spread that love to all you meet. Try to see Jesus in the poor one in front of you. And let God use you any way He wants to. Are you eating properly?"

"Yes." I didn't dare complain about the food I was getting at the Y. She patted my arm and said, "You look healthy." I didn't know if she was a referring to my size or to the blush on my cheeks. "Now it's time for Adoration." We walked up the stairs together. At the doorway of the chapel Mother genuflected on both knees, made the Sign of the Cross and then entered. Once in her spot she knelt again and bowed her forehead to the floor.

I watched her with new interest. She stayed on her knees through the entire Rosary, which took about half an hour. I collapsed to a sitting position after reciting a couple of decades, but I noticed I was able to kneel for longer periods.

I left the Mother House buoyant; Mother had talked to me, and she was very human. I had seen several sides of her in a short space of time: her irritation, her generosity of spirit, her practicality, and her devotion. She seemed to have complete self-acceptance and a tremendous ability to pay attention to what was in front of her. As I strolled along Rippon Street taking in the throbbing life all about me, I reflected how lucky I was to be having this experience.

1976 had been a momentous year for me. America celebrated its Bicentennial; I became the first woman art auctioneer and an American citizen; I saw my father for the last time, and I got divorced. But most significant of all, it was the year I came face-to-face with myself and admitted I had a drinking problem.

A series of events led up to this revelation. First, after my marriage had ended there was a brief but obsessive romance with a much older man. I had hoped to marry this man though he hadn't asked me or even mentioned it—a minor wrinkle. What attracted me to him was not his fine character or his love for me, neither of which was evident. He did, however, have the one thing in the world I wanted—he had a maid. I longed for a maid. I wanted someone to wake me up, fix my meals, lay out my clothes, brush my hair, and tuck me into bed.

In his apartment, every chair I settled in had next to it a side table with a box of loose cigarettes, a lighter and an ashtray. I was always looking for one or all three of those items, and to be able to flop into any chair and have them right at hand was heaven. The lover himself was barely relevant. I was, by now, so shut down emotionally that in order to have access to a maid, I was willing to entertain thoughts of a life with this fellow and to allow him to touch the sacred temple! In some circles this would be called prostitution.

That summer I attended a convention in London sponsored by Sotheby's, and after it was over, I had arranged to join the lover in Paris. One evening during the convention, there was a dinner and dance at a smart hotel. I pulled myself together for this grand event and even managed to look quite elegant in a long, midnight blue Grecian gown held on one shoulder with an orange Bakelite pin I always wore.

While couples were dancing, I went from table to table and poured half-empty drinks into my own glass. I knew something was wrong. I could see my behavior didn't exactly match my dress or my Sotheby's title, but I couldn't stop myself. I was sure no one noticed me; they were busy dancing, I told myself. Besides it was none of their business. But however much I excused my actions to myself, a nagging doubt persisted. I retaliated against my judgment by telling myself, "I don't give a damn what they think," or "I'm different," or "These people are so square they wouldn't understand anyway."

My duties in London completed, I hopped on a plane for Paris. The assignation was a disaster. My lover acted as if he didn't want me there at all. I felt awkward and out of place. Within thirty-six hours I was on a plane back to London. I was miserable, so miserable I couldn't enjoy being with my parents, even for a day. I told them I wanted to return to New York to be in America for the Bicentennial. It was the last time I was to see my father. He was standing by the garden gate smiling and waving good-bye, but I was too wrapped up in myself to pay much attention. The memory still haunts me and fills me with regret.

On July third, back in New York, I felt alone and alienated. I so wanted to see the Tall Ships come into New York Harbor. They had come from all over the world to sail up the Hudson as part of the Bicentennial celebration, but I never made it. The weather was superb, the mood in the city ebullient, festive—a mood I saw, heard, understood but couldn't feel. Something inside me was dying.

My Obsession returned from Paris a few weeks later and invited me for brunch the next day. From an emotional cave, I agreed. I woke up in a state of dread about the date. I wanted a drink. I fixed a jug of vodka and orange juice and poured myself a large glass. The liquid glided down my throat. The warm glow of the alcohol reached my stomach and spread lovingly through my aching system offering a sense of well-being and ease. The effect was immediate, as always. My soul sighed with relief, "Thank God.

I can keep it together and get through another day." The plastic wall melted away. Alcohol did the trick.

Then it suddenly dawned on me that I was drinking in the morning. I even said to myself in a tone of wonder, "This is a morning drink. I am drinking in the morning," as though having a drink in the morning was a rare and amazing happening. There is an Oriental saying, "The beginning of wisdom is to call something by its correct name." Now, I had had drinks in the morning many, many times, but I never called it "drinking in the morning." I called it "brunch" or "gallery openings" or "toasting the bride"; there were innumerable names to call it. For some reason, this time was different. This time I called it by its correct name and said, "This is a morning drink." But hot on the heels of the truth a voice whispered, "Oh, Lorna, what a fool you've been. You always make things so difficult for yourself. The sort of woman you are, with the problems you have to deal with. You have such a full plate. You deserve a little help. Why don't you give yourself a break? Why don't you have a drink every morning? Life would be so much easier."

I agreed wholeheartedly. I poured myself another. From that moment on I could not put the glass down. The glass and my hand were one. I got into the shower with it clutched in one hand while soaping myself with the other, trying to keep the precious liquid out of the spray. I had another revelation, "It's not that you don't want to put the glass down, you can't put it down." I believe God saw me weaving about in the shower and took pity.

I was drunk when I arrived for the brunch, and I drank more. The lover and I argued. Vowing never to see him again, I walked home. It was hot. My hair was braided too tightly and gave me a headache. At home I polished off the jug from the morning and passed out. When I came to, I reached for the telephone and called Sister Rosemary.

Some months before, a friend had given me Sister Rosemary's number saying if I ever needed help or someone to talk to,

Sister Rosemary was the person to call. At the time I couldn't imagine ever wanting to talk to a nun about anything of a personal nature, but nevertheless, I had put her number in my wallet. A pleasant-sounding woman came to the telephone; I can't remember what I said. I think I cried. She invited me to come over right then.

Once in the Marymount convent on East 72nd Street, I had the same feeling of safety and order I had known at Gumley. Sister Rosemary was in her mid-sixties; she had a stocky build and a broad smiling face—she conveyed an air of robust practicality. She wore a short white habit and veil, and with her scrubbed face and brawny arms, it seemed she could wrestle any problem into submission; nothing would be permitted to daunt her spirit. I found myself spilling out all the details of the love affair and told her that because I was so unhappy, I'd had lot to drink that day. When I was through, she looked at me keenly and said, "My dear, it sounds as though you have a drinking problem. Here's what I suggest you do. . . ."

She was way off base; drinking wasn't my problem— my problem was no one understood me. My friends, my broken marriage, the lover—those were my problems, not drinking. Drinking was my comfort, my friend. But other forces were working. In spite of my feelings, I agreed to follow Sister Rosemary's suggestions.

She directed me to a basement in the Moravian Church on Lexington Avenue where people met regularly to talk about their drinking. When I walked in, the snob in me surfaced. "This place is the pits. What am I doing? I don't belong here." But I couldn't leave; I was still slightly tipsy and too self-conscious to leave. So with an attitude of pained endurance, I plopped myself into a chair and sat with people I thought were neither my peers nor my class. But mixed in with feelings of superiority was a fragile awareness I did belong— that these were my people. I flip-flopped; suddenly I was scared they wouldn't want me, and I'd be asked to leave. In truth, I had nowhere else to go.

A woman started speaking. She wasn't pretty; her face was ruddy with broken capillaries on her nose and cheeks, but she was sober. She was telling her story and mine. She talked about her childhood fears of abandonment and of being sent away, about leaving home early, about a terrible marriage to a man she thought artistic but who always cheated on her, about a successful career, about her own bad behavior when drinking. She said she had had alcoholic attitudes as a child: that even before she picked up her first drink, she was an alcoholic waiting to happen. She arrived at the stage in her life where I stood, and then she went on. For another fifteen years she went on. I looked at her with fascination and horror; I was transfixed. It seemed to me we were the same person. Here was God in the form of what looked to me to be a hag, allowing me to see what I could become.

It felt it was no accident I was in that room, that a divine hand had orchestrated events and that indeed probably my whole life had been a preparation for being able to "hear" this woman. All in a rush, wonder and relief swept over me as I realized my life wasn't a mess because of my childhood, my marriage, my job or any relationship. It was a mess because I drank.

I couldn't stop drinking by myself. I needed help. Over the next weeks I found myself in similar rooms in the midst of many others like me, each one with an awareness about their drinking, each a testament of hope. I learned I had a disease, a self-diagnosed disease, a disease called alcoholism. I learned that alcoholism was a disease of the attitudes, a disease of denial, despair and isolation. I also learned there was a solution. Alcoholism, I was told, could not be cured, only arrested, one day at a time. The people I met shared with me all their feelings of uselessness and despair. I was not unique. I was not alone.

My life began to open in a way I'd never dreamed possible. I was suddenly on a completely different track. I developed new friendships. If I stayed sober, my new friends assured me, I would get better and better. The quality I had been looking for, the quality that had been sparked in me at Gumley and again when I walked into Sotheby's could now be explored; I could come into my own. All my life I'd heard, "Lorna, you're too much." Now I was being encouraged, "Why don't you try becoming more of who you really are?"

I'd been given a great gift, I'd been touched by grace. I was reminded of a few lines from a poem by Gerald Manley Hopkins,

> *. . . there lives the dearest freshness deep down things . . .*
> *And though the last lights off the black West went*
> *Oh, morning, at the brown brink eastward, springs*
> *Because the Holy Ghost over the bent*
> *World broods with warm breast and with ah! bright wings.*

I was sober and I was in Calcutta, India. I had met Mother Teresa. I waved at the yogurt man and he waved back.

Tuesday,
March 24, 1981

Mother Teresa acknowledged me with a nod and a smile when I entered the chapel; I all but died with delight. After Mass she took me aside and inquired about my plans for the day. When she spoke to me, I felt I was the only person in the world for her at that moment. I told her Sister Paulette had invited Etienne and me to go to a village with her to learn about the Natural Family Planning program.

"*Acha, acha,* Sister Paulette does a great work. You should learn a lot." Then, quite abruptly she asked, "Are you Catholic?" The sudden switch in topics and her directness threw me.

"Well, I was baptized Catholic," I sighed, "but I don't know if I'm really Catholic. I don't know how I feel about the Virgin Birth; I don't understand devotion to the Sacred Heart of Jesus; I don't like the Pope and . . . ."

Mother cut me off, waving her hand impatiently as if flicking away gnats, "Oh you're Catholic!" That was that. All my posturing brushed aside with a stroke of her hand. In an odd way I found Mother's attitude comforting—it confirmed what I had always suspected, that once a Catholic, always a Catholic, and part of being Catholic is to have trouble with Catholicism. It reminded me of an experience I'd had shortly after becoming an American citizen.

I was returning to England for a visit carrying both my British and my new American passport. When I went through immigration, I anxiously asked the official which passport he wanted to see. He leaned forward on his elbows, looked me straight in the eye and said, "Listen, luv, you can become anything you like, but as far as we're concerned, you're British."

Etienne and I hurried to Prem Dan to meet Sister Paulette. She was waiting for us. She looked odd—her kerchief and veil were askew, pushed back and up one side of her head, giving her a rakish appearance. As a sign of modesty, a Missionaries of Charity sister wears her head covering pulled forward, almost to the eyebrows, so Paulette wearing her veil like a reversed baseball cap was highly unorthodox, although I found it endearing.

We left Prem Dan and headed for the railroad station. As we walked across the tracks I thought about the woman who had jumped from the bridge, and I shuddered. Paulette dashed ahead to get the tickets. When the train arrived, I stood aside to let the scrambling hordes pass, but Sister Paulette grabbed me, pushed and shoved and elbowed her way forward, propelling me ahead of her. She had no inhibitions whatsoever about barging through a knot of people. She behaved more like a fullback for the New York Giants than a nun.

As on the buses, there was a Women's Section, and Paulette almost did physical damage to a couple of women to make sure we got a seat. I felt a little awkward as I sat on the bench taking up the space of about three women, not that I was enormous, but they were so compact and seemed to be able to squeeze themselves into the smallest cranny. I made an attempt to give up my spot, but Paulette insisted in a loud voice that I remain seated.

The coach interior was dark and dirty with creaking overhead fans and wooden seats—getting a seat next to an open window was every passenger's goal. There were no doors, and many commuters stood or squatted by the openings. Some of the younger men hung outside the coaches, grasping at anything that afforded a handhold. Sellers of sweets, fruits, nuts, hair ornaments, sponges and a riot of other trinkets and edibles made their way through the carriages, hawking their wares. A blind couple, holding out their hands for coins, squeezed through the press of passengers, singing as they went.

We rode squashed and uncomfortable for almost an hour, then piled off at a siding and began a short walk down a winding path past bamboo groves, palm trees and over irrigation trenches. Mynah birds and sparrows replaced the chorus of crows; the air was sweet and cool; jasmine and bougainvillea flourished. As we approached the village, the children, like monkeys, darted and danced ahead of us chattering with excitement, announcing our arrival.

We crossed a bridge over a fetid pond; women were on their knees washing pots and doing laundry in the murky water. Close by children swam and splashed about, shrieking, having a wonderful time. The village itself was a conglomeration of shacks with dirt floors no more than twelve by fifteen feet. The walls were made of corrugated metal, straw matting, plastic and any other material that offered protection; the roofs of layered plastic and odd bits were no match for the monsoons. Paulette told us that from mid-June to mid-September the occupants were constantly wet or, at the very least, damp. For the pleasure of living in these hovels, the villagers had to pay rent to a *zamindar* (landlord).

Every home we entered was neat and well-ordered.

There were nearly always calendar pictures of Krishna and other deities: Lakshmi, goddess of prosperity; Ganesh, elephant-headed god of good fortune; Hanuman the monkey god—all adorned with floral garlands. I was surprised to see pictures of Jesus and Mary in many of the homes. Paulette explained that Jesus and Mary are considered to be powerful saints by many Hindus and are highly revered.

Everywhere we went we were treated like honored guests. The three of us were much larger than the average Indian, so when we were all inside one of the single-room dwellings, there was little room to spare. I had to tread carefully; I was sure that if I stumbled against one of the walls of palm fronds, plastic and clay, I might bring down a whole row of houses. Mats were scattered on the floor to sit upon, but we were asked to, *please* sit on the low bed, a place of honor and usually the only piece of furniture.

Neighbors gathered and crowded around the doorway. We were offered tea or lemonade to drink but always declined. One of the tenets of the Missionaries of Charity Constitution is not to partake of food or drink while outside the convent. This is not only in deference to the poor but also for health considerations.

Paulette questioned the wives who were part of the program; she asked them how they were feeling, how life was treating them. She examined the scrap of paper which doubled as a crude monthly chart; on it the woman noted with an X her dry and fertile days. Many women were anemic and we gave them vitamins. Etienne rallied the children for a checkup. If they had worms—most did—we handed out special pills tucked into envelopes fashioned from old newspapers.

After we had finished our rounds, we found a shady spot outdoors. Paulette gathered the women about her and instructed new candidates, mostly girls about to be married. Young boys tried to hang around the periphery and were shooed away. Sister Paulette took an intense interest in the lives of the women she helped, and it was fascinating to watch her sitting among them explaining the program and to watch the women listen to her with rapt attention.

I liked this work. I liked the whole idea of teaching. It was more inspiring to me than cleaning wounds and dealing with the sick. Sometimes when I walked into Kalighat, I had an insane urge to clap my hands and say, "All right, all right, we'll have no more dying today—all this dying simply has to stop!"

On the train going home Paulette managed to secure seats for us both while Etienne stood near the door. We had a wonderful chat. She talked about her family in Mauritius and about her "call" to be a nun. She'd been toying with the idea for a while, she told me, when one day, at the age of eighteen, whilst she was walking on a beach near her hometown, she felt the presence of Jesus. He was walking with her, showing her beautiful shells on the shore and talking to her softly as a lover would. She knew she had been called, and she wanted, with all her heart, to respond to the call and live a life as His spouse. She talked with great rapture about her ever-deepening love affair with Jesus, and she didn't seem to be the slightest bit concerned everyone around was listening. She said, "Like any marriage, marriage with Jesus is sometimes hard. He can be very demanding." Then she wanted to know about me and how I'd come to be in Calcutta.

I told her about my job, and she boldly asked how much money I earned. She almost dropped dead when I told her. It wasn't a large amount by any stretch of an American imagination; in fact like many women I was underpaid, but it sounded like a king's ransom when translated into rupees. For someone who had taken a vow of poverty, she was mighty interested in money and fascinated with the lives of the wealthy. I indulged her.

"Visiting the homes of the rich is one of the highlights of my job." I told her about Edith Whetmore's bedroom at Chateau Sur Mer, in Newport, Rhode Island, " . . . decorated in pale hues to set off the European furnishings. The dressing-table chair in her *boudoir* was the very same chair upon which Marie-Antoinette sat the royal posterior when powdering the royal nose at Versailles—the only difference being Edith added a homey touch by sandwiching some old pillow between herself and the historic seat."

I couldn't help thinking what a far cry Edith's home was from the hovels I'd just visited. "We would often tiptoe about," I continued, "prying into every nook and cranny, hoping to unearth a forgotten treasure. 'Dear Lord,' we silently prayed, 'please, a Rembrandt hanging in the carriage house would be nice, or maybe a fragment from the great palace of Persepolis now used as a doorstop.' Our fantasies ran riot."

The train was pulling into the station; I promised to tell her more stories some other day. Paulette had to hurry back to the Mother House. Etienne and I thanked her, and as we made our way back to the Y, the sky suddenly clouded over. We hadn't gone thirty paces when the heavens opened, soaking us in a matter of moments. Dashing through the downpour, I thought how lucky I was to have a dry room to sleep in and dry clothes to wear; the villagers we had visited would not be so fortunate. It poured for ten minutes—then stopped abruptly. The rain cooled the city momentarily, but soon the atmosphere grew humid again, and every surface steamed.

After lunch I went to a bank to change traveler's checks. At least five officials had to see my passport. They examined it so intently I wondered if they thought I was a spy. Each official signed and stamped a triplicate form then directed me to stand in line to see the next one. Finally I made it to the cashier's grille. When I had finished this maddening two-hour experience, I was in a murderous mood. I wanted to pummel each bank employee; instead I took myself off to a local beauty parlor for a massage and let someone pummel me. Then, still bent on hedonistic pursuits, I flopped into Flury's for cake and coffee.

The weather was strange. Normally by the early evening, it was swelteringly hot and still, but this evening during the Rosary the rain sheeted down again, accompanied by a howling wind. The unwelcome wind entered the chapel and whipped around us, causing the shutters to chatter and making it almost impossible to concentrate. Why didn't one of the sisters get up and close the windows? I felt it wasn't my place to make such a move. Finally, Mother entered and asked in a rather exasperated voice, "Are you mad? What are you thinking of? Why don't you close the windows?" Several sisters jumped up at once and latched the wooden shutters.

Halfway through the Rosary one of the Swiss volunteers came into chapel and, in an effort to have a good view of Mother, practically sat down of top of me. I felt murderous all over again and wished I had a large hatpin to jab in her bottom, but I did nothing and even managed to hold my tongue. What was the matter with me? Here I was in this wonderfully Christian atmosphere a few feet away from a woman the world considered a saint, and I was beset with barbarous and vicious thoughts. I seemed to be getting worse not better.

I felt not a little triumphant when, in front of the Swiss heffalump, Mother called me aside and asked how my day had been. I told her about the village and Sister Paulette and then about my experience at the bank. "It was such a rigmarole of red tape anyone would have thought I was signing the Magna Carta instead of a few traveler's checks." She chuckled. I did not mention the massage or Flury's cake shop.

Following a cherished national ritual, that evening after dinner, I sat on the verandah having a cup of tea with other British volunteers. It had been a long day.

Wednesday,
March 25, 1981

It happened again! At Mass the Swiss woman who tried to push me aside at Adoration yesterday evening just plonked herself down, this time on my foot! I prayed to God to let my annoyance subside, but He must have been busy in China or some other place because He did not hear me.

"Well, really, do you mind? That's my foot!" I tutted in an exasperated tone of voice, right there in the middle of Mass with Mother able to hear every word.

Why was I so impatient? I had thought being around so much suffering would make me tolerant. No such luck.

After Mass Mother indicated I should wait for her while she greeted the visitors. I leaned over the balcony and looked into the yard and watched, fascinated, as I had that first morning, the sisters doing their laundry. There was no talking but much clanking, swooshing and slapping.

Soon Mother joined me. She wanted to know about my life in New York—what I did for a living. I told her about being in the art business and about becoming an auctioneer. She was not too sure what an auctioneer was and made me explain it in more detail. I rattled off a few figures, and gestured with my hands, "At five-thousand, five-thousand dollars on my left at five-thousand. Five-thousand two-hundred in the rear now. Five-thousand-four hundred, thank you madam. Will you say five-thousand-six sir?

No, are you sure? At five-thousand-four hundred then, the lady's bid, are you all through? Fair warning. . . ."

Smack! I slapped my palm on the smooth edge of the balcony, "Sold to the lady in the rear."

Mother reflected for a moment and said, "Ah, yes. You know, they have a lot of that art stuff in the Vatican!" Then she zeroed in; I had known it was coming; it was only a matter of time: "Are you married?"

I decided to keep it simple. "I was married, but I've been divorced for six years." I must have been whistling Dixie if I thought she'd let me get away with just that.

"Couldn't you get back with your husband?"

"No, I wouldn't want to."

"Why did you get divorced?"

Even though I knew Mother would never be judgmental, I felt uneasy and not a little embarrassed. I honestly didn't feel like relating the whole sordid story, the betrayals, the drinking, the fights. But looking at her, this diminutive woman with her sensible face and worldly eyes, I felt I would be hard put to tell her something she hadn't heard before. "My marriage ended because of alcoholism. I'm an alcoholic. I've been in recovery for four-and-a-half years."

Mother stood leaning against the balcony, her head slightly to one side. She reached out her hand and covered mine. "You mean you don't drink any more?"

"No, I don't drink at all."

"How beautiful." She turned her focus away from the divorce and seemed to be captivated by the fact I had drunk, had had a problem with it, and didn't drink now. She wanted to know more. I tried to explain:

"When I came down the assembly line in Heaven, God said, 'I have yearned for you to love me. I have waited so long for you. This time you're going to long for me too;

this time you're going to be mine.' And He stamped **ALCOHOLIC** on my soul so that eventually, in my helplessness, and despair, I would turn to Him."

Mother liked my imagery. "How beautiful," she said again. Then she asked if I ever felt like drinking and if I found being in Calcutta difficult.

I told her that although I rarely craved alcohol, I would always have alcoholism—a disease that wants me to drink again. I had been taught to "think the drink through." Nevertheless I still had to be careful about mood swings. Then I confessed my feelings about Calcutta—feelings of despair at seeing such poverty and suffering. How I had expected to be moved by compassion, but how instead I seemed to be getting harder not softer. I told her my experience with the volunteer at Mass that very morning. Mother laughed and said she had witnessed the episode but not to worry; it was normal to feel irritated and upset.

She said Calcutta was hard for Westerners to absorb, and I probably had underestimated how much it was affecting me. She felt it was important for the volunteers to occasionally take themselves to The Grand, a top hotel, to indulge themselves in familiar comforts. Calcutta and the work of the Missionaries of Charity, she said, was a culture shock and stressful. She said she could not possibly do the work for even one day without her spiritual discipline and daily Eucharist. She recognized it was hard for volunteers who didn't have the same vocation or the sisters' intense spiritual practice or their communal support.

I felt relaxed and more inclined to tell her about yesterday afternoon, about the massage and Flury's. She responded with, "*Acha, acha.*" She stroked my arm and said not to worry about irritations. "God loves all of you. Offer everything, good and bad to Him. I'll say some special prayers for you. God has brought you here for a reason. He'll open your heart in His time, not yours."

I left her, and I walked to the British Airways ticket office to confirm my homebound flight only to discover my worst fears realized. I was informed my flight to London did not even exist. How could that be? I had booked the flight through a reputable travel agent in New York. What did they mean it didn't exist? Mother's words about God's bringing me here for a reason were gone in an instant. Again I experienced the same projected horrors of being trapped in Calcutta. I felt tempted to go straight to the airport and fly the plane out myself! The ticket agent could tell he was not dealing with a rational being who was able to accept the news of a delay with equanimity. He assured me that although flights out of Calcutta were nearly always full, he would try to book me on a flight in a week and backed up his promise with another flight. I calmed down. I had to let God run the show; I did hope He knew what He was doing. I distracted myself by going back to Prem Dan.

Meeta's wounds still needed to be dressed daily, but they continued to improve. I marveled at her recovery. There were large scabs forming in some areas and the smell had diminished. Sister Veronica and I lifted her and took her outside into the yard to get some fresh air; we put her in the shade of a sprawling tree.

Outside, many of the other patients were clustered in groups, taking in the air. All of a sudden I looked up and saw one old woman alone and writhing on the ground. I hurried over to her. She had had an attack of diarrhea and been violently sick, and in her vain attempts to get up, had rolled around in the mess. She was covered with vomit and excrement, down her legs, her back, her front, in her hair. I certainly didn't want to touch her and get the muck all over myself, so I tried tentatively to hold an edge of her sodden gown in order make her stand so that I could walk her back to the ward to be hosed off. She tried, but she couldn't stand, let alone walk. Her legs collapsed and she landed back in her filth. Irritation welled up again. I looked at her with disgust. Then I did what I had done countless times in one form or another, I turned my back on her and I walked away. "It's all too much. I didn't come here for this. It's not my problem." I said to myself, "Why should I deal with the mess? Let someone else take care of her."

I had gone just a few yards when I thought, "Supposing that poor, sick woman was my mother. How would I feel if someone capable of helping *my* mother were to turn her back and walk away?" I did not like that thought. It was distressing to visualize my own mother sick, in need, abandoned. But still I continued to walk away. Then it struck me: indeed this woman *was* my mother. She was everyone's mother. She was Jesus in the disguise of a broken, smelly old woman. The truth of Mother Teresa's oft-quoted statement hit me, "See Jesus in the distressing disguise of the poor and suffering."

If this were the filthy, battered body of Jesus taken down from the cross, would I walk away? I heard a resounding "No." I felt such shame and resolution. I rushed back, and plunging through my repulsion, scooped her up into my arms like a baby. Holding her close, I carried her inside the women's pavilion to the washroom. I held my breath as I reeled through the doors. She was like a damaged, bony bird in my arms, and I could feel her fear. My heart cracked open. I felt the shift. I washed her with care and loving attention.

After I'd put her to bed and cleaned myself, I sat on the low wall that lined the path to the main gate. The courtyard was a bizarre sight with numerous old women perambulating in slow motion. Many of them wailed and moaned, a sort of perpetual keening, and a number of them waddled along like ducks, very close to the ground. These poor souls had not one ounce of spare flesh on their withered frames and had spent their lives squatting so that now their backs were permanently bent, and standing was difficult. All of them had the same haunted look in their eyes—their struggles etched on their faces. How did these women end up here? Did they have children? What had they seen in their lives? What did they know?

I stopped at Paulette's office, and we walked back to the Mother House together. She said she had eaten with Mother Teresa the night before and had told Mother all about me, about my job in America, how much money I earned. "She was so interested; I'm sure she'll talk to you."

"Paulette, she already has this morning. I was wondering why the sudden interest, and why she was pumping me for information. I ended up telling her I'd been married and about my being an alcoholic; it was quite a conversation."

"You were married? My lord, I didn't realize you were married. What do you mean you're an alcoholic? How much do you drink?"

"Well, by God's grace I don't drink anymore."

"How beautiful." She used the same words Mother had. "Did you drink when you were working at that important job?"

"I was never rolling around drunk that I know of, but sometimes I'd have a few drinks at lunch, and I'd be tipsy and slurring my words in the afternoon. My alcoholism had manifested itself mostly in feelings of low self-esteem, in my behavior and in the way I dressed."

"Go on."

"Are you sure you want to hear all this?"

"Yes, I'm fascinated."

So I told her. Even though I had a good job and was good at what I did, I had felt no amount of praise could entirely expel the feeling I had of being a phony, that I was really just winging the whole thing. Those feelings were always with me to some degree, ebbing and flowing, a nagging, destructive current. It was only a matter of time before I would be exposed for the impostor I felt I was. I had been minimally aware I was losing my grip, and I desperately wanted my "outsides" at least, to look "very together."

I was finding even the most mundane tasks were becoming too much to handle. I had long hair; most women with long hair choose to have it long because they enjoy it, but for me, my long hair was nothing but torture. I wore it pulled straight back off my face in a bun, or in braids across the top of my head. This way I could keep it up for two or three days at a time without having to bother with it; I was trying to find a "forever" hairstyle. I fancied I looked like Heidi, but I probably looked more like du Maurier's Mrs. Danvers. Paulette didn't get this reference, and I thought it just too complicated to explain.

I went on. I had not had any obvious, bell-clanging awareness about my alcoholism—no hospitals, no drying-out farms, just a slow disintegration of my spirit. The only hints I had, and I did not recognize them as signs of a drinking problem, were the constant negative feelings. My behavior, fueled by alcohol, was becoming more and more outrageous. I didn't know what I would say or do next, or how I would dress for a function. I put on stockings with runs, thinking people would assume I'd torn them that minute. I could afford new stockings every day, but I never got around to buying them. I wore the same outfit day after day. I couldn't be bothered to think of a new ensemble and pull it together.

At one time I had enjoyed shopping in thrift shops; it was something I had done with flair. I did have to stop and explain to Paulette what a thrift shop was. It was anathema to her that people would give away perfectly good clothes for a tax deduction.

I proceeded with my tale. I might find an unusual handbag or maybe a great jacket in a thrift shop, but then I began to shop in them all the time. It was easier to pick up someone else's discarded clothes than face a big department store; I found it too overwhelming. I had reached a point where I didn't even care too much about the condition of the thrift shop clothes. If it fit, I bought it. On one occasion I asked a friend what she thought of my new dress. She stared at it for a long time then said, "Well, Lorna, the color's pretty, but there are cigarette burns down the front of it."

"Can you really see them?" I asked. I had known the holes were there when I'd purchased it, but had hoped they wouldn't show. "Perhaps not, if I were sitting on the opposite side of a football stadium from you," she replied.

Another time at work, a colleague took me aside and, not wanting to embarrass me, very gently and kindly inquired, "Lorna, why are you wearing a maid's uniform?" As soon as she said it, I could see it was indeed a maid's uniform. It had a little round white collar with matching cuffs and a belt of the same fabric. I had selected it at the thrift shop thinking it made me look neat and tidy. When people came to Sotheby's to have their items appraised, it's a wonder they didn't give me their coat to hang up. More than a few must have been surprised to discover that I was, in fact, the expert who was to help them with their collections.

I didn't fit in; my timing was wrong; I was always making inappropriate remarks, laughing too loudly and at the wrong times. No one ever realized my drinking was out of hand;

instead they made comments like "You're awfully spiteful," or "That was very hurtful; what you think is amusing is really unkind," or "Shush, please, shush." I had little awareness of my descent, but as I descended, the next step didn't look so far, nor the next. Things I swore I would never do were becoming commonplace. My standards didn't suddenly plunge—they eroded. I was constantly having to adjust my values to suit the new, lower situation.

Paulette was listening intently. We strolled sedately through the streets together, passing through the extraordinary scenes that make up daily life in Calcutta—like two duchesses at a village fair—oblivious to the frenzied pace around them. "Did you ever take any drugs?" she suddenly asked.

"Yes."

"Tell me what taking drugs is like."

We were a few blocks away from the Mother House. A cart carrying sacks of cabbages had broken a wheel, and the cabbages were strewn all over. The frantic owners were scrambling to retrieve their vegetables and to clear the road.

"Well, the drug I liked the very best was Acid—LSD. It was absolutely fantastic, and it really did 'blow my mind.' I never had what is called 'a bad trip'; I was lucky. I never felt more sane than when I was on Acid, never felt more in the moment, more in the 'now.' " I got carried away and forgot I was talking to a nun. "And making love on Acid, well, that was something else. It felt as if we were one and that the lovemaking could last forever."

"Ah," murmured Paulette dreamily. "What Heaven must be like!"

The cabbage men cleared the street, and we passed on to Adoration.

Thursday,
March 26, 1981

This morning I boarded a train with three other volunteers to visit the Leper center at Titagarh, just a short distance from Calcutta. My companions were French girls in their early twenties who had come to Calcutta as a group to meet Mother Teresa and to work for a few months.

Wherever I went, I seemed to attract attention. I'm sure most of the people who came in contact with the Missionaries of Charity thought me an oddity. I tried to see myself as they might see me—European or American, obviously young in spite of graying hair. I was tall by Indian standards, and they probably found my red lipstick and red nails either glamorous or outrageous. I certainly did not look like the other women volunteers who eschewed makeup of any description. Often a group would gather to stare at me, not in a threatening or unkind way, but with curiosity. While we were sitting on the platform waiting for the train, I unzipped the pouch around my waist and produced my mirror and lipstick. Within seconds a crowd circled me, some literally inches from my face, watching my every move as I applied the lipstick.

When the train pulled in, we all scrambled aboard. I wasn't as good at claiming a seat as Paulette, so we had to stand for most of the forty-minute journey. The leprosy rehabilitation center, Gandhiji Prem Nivas (Gandhi Center of Love), was a short walk from the station. The Missionary

Brothers of Charity who ran it tended to almost three hundred inpatients and hundreds more outpatients.

Brother Christos was in charge. A short, energetic man in his mid-forties, he was a Missionaries of Charity priest and a fully qualified doctor specializing in leprosy. He was possessed of a God-given optimism and laughed a great deal, not gratuitously but from genuine joy which emanated from his whole being.

He was a very busy man, but he seemed delighted to see us and show us around. The center, he said, had become almost self-sufficient. The main industry at Titagarh was the manufacturing of cotton, and besides making fabric for commercial use, the lepers wove all the cotton goods the Missionaries of Charity used: enormous quantities of bed sheets as well as the cloth they used to make their own habits and saris.

We entered one of several long sheds. At one end, patients were squatting on the ground at spinning wheels, taking the cotton and spinning it into cotton skeins for dyeing. Along each side of the shed, facing the center, was a row of hand-and-foot-operated weaving looms. There was a constant clacking as the wooden shuttle was passed from one side of the cloth to the other and a thwacking sound as the baton of wood was thrust up against the fabric to mesh the warp with the woof. Miles and miles of cotton fabric, plain, intricately checkered and variously patterned, were produced by these old-fashioned methods. Just outside the sheds were huge tubs of vivid dyes, and skeins of brightly colored cotton hung out to dry in the sun.

The scope of Mother Teresa's vision was evident in this thriving community. It was all so exquisitely simple. Hundreds of handicapped people who would otherwise have been reduced to begging on the streets had found employment and had been able to develop a measure of pride and self-esteem. Men and women busily manipulated looms and spinning wheels despite missing fingers and toes.

The Titagarh community supported many families. There were individual homes and even a school for the very young children. There were several workshops; the one that most appealed to me was a cobbler's where the lepers fashioned sandals out of old car tires. Brother Christos explained that when the disease attacked the feet, sandals had to be custom-made to accommodate those who had lost toes or had only a stump where once a whole foot had been. He added that the lepers in this workshop made the sandals Mother Teresa wore.

Once while on Molokai in the Hawaiian Islands, I rode a mule down an almost sheer cliff face to Kalapapa, the leper colony founded by Father Damien. Damien was a Belgian priest who, in the 19th century, dedicated his life to helping the lepers on Molokai. I remembered sitting in one of the tiny clapboard churches Damien had built and noticing holes, about three inches in diameter, bored into the floorboards at regular intervals. I couldn't imagine what they were for. I found the answer sometime later when I read a biography of Father Damien. The disease of leprosy produces a lot of phlegm, and the holes were drilled in the floorboards so that during Mass, those lepers with damaged feet, could spit where they sat and not have to make the painful walk outside. A typical saint, Damien had a reputation for being hot-tempered and blunt, but I thought the drilled holes revealed his sensitivity and practical compassion.

A garden on the grounds at Titagarh supplied vegetables for the community, and as we approached, one of the gardeners stopped his work; he was a skinny fellow who simply could not stop smiling. Most of his teeth were missing as were most of his toes and the tops of several fingers, but none of these limitations prevented him from hopping nimbly over the vegetables. With pride he pointed out his handiwork: neat rows of seedlings just breaking through the topsoil.

We then visited the hospital where some of the community residents helped the brothers take care of the bedridden. I walked around the ward saying hello to everyone; for those too sick to give the traditional *namaskar,* I touched their forehead and then mine. It was evident Brother Christos was well loved; everywhere we went patients touched his feet and pleaded with him to stay a while; the children clung to his arms and bounced along beside him laughing and wheedling for attention.

Brother Christos invited us for lunch at the brothers' house but said he still had work to do and would join us later. The others went off to explore on their own, but I walked across the railroad tracks to the outpatient clinic, where I sat with Brother Christos and watched as the stream of lepers came in for treatment.

A young woman arrived; she was about twenty years old, newly married and very distraught. She had leprosy in its early stages, numb patches on the forehead. A new bride, she was terrified her husband would discover her condition and divorce her. Brother Christos explained that if she took the prescribed medicine, the disease could be arrested and she would not have to suffer any of the common disfiguration or loss of digits; no one need ever know she had leprosy.

Once again I felt dismay. The vow of "in sickness and in health" did not apply for this young woman or for thousands like her. Her marriage had, of course, been arranged, and she feared her husband and his family. If they discovered she had leprosy, they would in all probability think they had received damaged goods and want a divorce. Maybe she was fearful of becoming another statistic in the bride-burning crime file. Brother Christos assured her that neither her husband nor his family need ever find out about her situation and that her treatment would be kept confidential. I watched her walk away, her pretty dark head bowed, her sari falling in graceful folds around her, the gold threads glinting in the sunlight, her arms clutched tightly about her as if to contain and protect her sorrowful secret.

When Brother Christos finished in the clinic, we strolled to the brothers' residence. It was in an old wooden house with external walkways and balconies; the interior was cool, sparse, and spotlessly clean. A crucifix and one or two religious pictures hung on the plain white walls in every room. The brothers lived a much less restricted life than their female counterparts, and they wore western clothes—the only thing distinguishing them as Religious was a small crucifix pinned to their shirts. Eight of them lived in the house, and I was struck by how young they all were.

Lunch was a simple affair of rice and *dal*, the chatter around the table light and lively; they were full of questions about the world outside Calcutta and were especially interested in sports, about which I knew not a thing.

Before we departed, much to our delight, Brother Christos invited us to join him a few days hence on a trip to Shanti Nagar, a Missionaries of Charity leper hospital and community about half a day's journey outside Calcutta. We said our good-byes and decided to return by bus—a big mistake. It was an endless hot journey on a crowded, stuffy vehicle with hard seats.

At the Mother House, Adoration had already begun. I took off my sandals and slipped quietly into the chapel. Mother smiled at me. I watched her in wonderment, reflecting on all I'd witnessed that day at Titagarh. This little old lady sitting on the floor could run General Motors, I thought. I watched her as she worshipped, her face a study in humility and concentration. Everything about her was loving: her look, her posture, even the way she fingered her rosary beads. She must have said the Rosary five zillion times, but as I watched those comfortable old hands caress each bead, it was as though she had just, in that very moment, discovered something wondrously new and beautiful she could offer to God.

There was another deluge; this time the sisters near the windows leapt to their feet and latched the shutters.

Friday,
March 27, 1981

This morning, during what had become our routine morning chats, Mother encouraged me to be holy and to live a life devoted to prayer and to listening to the will of God.

"Praying," she said, "opens the heart and increases our capacity to love." She often quoted Saint Teresa of Lisieux, whose name she had taken; Saint Teresa's short life was devoted to "doing small things with a great love." Mother spoke with wonder of the love of Jesus, "who could have come to us in any form, but chose the humblest of manifestations—the broken bread on the altar and the poorest of the poor."

I found myself drawn more and more by her directness, her simplicity, her deep devotion to Jesus and her unfaltering, magnetic faith. Whenever I left her, I suffered a sense of loss, as if I hadn't quite looked at her enough or listened to her enough or just simply been with her enough, and I found myself impatient for the next encounter. Today we talked a lot about our inner lives, or more accurately, we talked about *my* inner life. It was not easy to get Mother to open up about her own life. I recounted some childhood memories in an attempt to draw her out by talking about my own experiences. She was especially interested in the convent school I had attended and wanted to know about my mother.

My mother. . . I had mixed memories of my mother from childhood. A feisty, pretty woman, she had brilliant blue eyes and wore her long fair hair in an elegant flat bun on the top of her head. She took care with her appearance; I cannot ever remember seeing her sloppily attired. I received confusing messages from her. Sometimes, after she'd severely walloped me because I'd been naughty or rude, she'd send me to bed, and then, sobbing and feeling contrite, would come to my room and fling herself into my lap, and I'd find myself stroking her head and comforting her when I was the one in need.

I stopped at this point and looked at Mother Teresa. She smiled and nodded for me to continue.

I told her that when I was fourteen my parents contemplated sending me to a boarding school. My mother's twin sister, Aunt Lorna, who was living in Canada, learned of the plan and wrote: "Don't send her to boarding school. Why don't you send her to me for a year?" This offer was presented as a wonderful opportunity, and I also thought how lucky I was to have the chance to go to school abroad. I had a rude awakening.

My aunt was very intimidating. She was tall and forbidding, authoritarian and eccentric. Living with her meant enduring a succession of loud imperatives, criticisms and corrections. Her dress sense, too, was rather peculiar; she favored tailored suits with white blouses and pearls, but she'd ruin the look by carrying a child's beaded string bag and donning a balding fur cape. She wore long white kid gloves with little buttons, no longer fashionable and completely impractical for shopping at the supermarket. She had a penchant for lacy lingerie, all of which she meticulously washed and ironed by hand. Even in the hot Canadian summers, she would encase herself in a waist-length whalebone strapless bra that hooked up the front, like those of bar-room girls in Westerns. She wore a full slip, plus a half-slip and, although very slender, never went without a girdle.

The fifteen months I spent with my Aunt were a horror and the unhappiest period of my childhood. I felt beaten down and could make no friends. Speaking with an accent, I felt out of place at school, and so in some attempt to hold on to what was familiar to me, I wore my English school uniform, which only served to separate me further. I suspected my classmates thought me odd because I lived with my aunt and not my parents. I became lonely and withdrawn.

Deep down I suspected I was having a terrible time because I was a terrible person, and if I'd been better, my parents wouldn't have sent me away. When the sojourn in Canada was almost over, my mother telephoned and suggested I ask my aunt if I could stay another year. I became hysterical at the thought of my mother quite content not to see me for another twelve months. She had no idea why I was so upset. I'd never written to say I was unhappy, just the reverse. I had written glowing letters so my parents would believe I was having a wonderful time and not think me ungrateful.

A look of distress crossed Mother Teresa's face as I finished my saga. "Our mothers are truly blessings," she said. I couldn't believe my ears. I'd just related, albeit with more than a little self-pity, a story of what I considered to be abuse and abandonment, and now Mother Teresa was telling me I should consider my mother a blessing. This was too much. I couldn't stop the hurt and hostility I felt.

"I don't believe you," I shot back. "Don't tell me your relationship with your mother was so great. After all, you left home when you were eighteen." Now Mother fixed me with stern, resolute eyes, and in a slow, steady voice tinged with just the right amount of anger, replied, "Leaving my mother was the greatest sacrifice of my life."

I apologized immediately and felt terrible for having been so rude.

Why hadn't I just kept my mouth shut?

I joined Sister Paulette on a mission to a slum area she hadn't visited before. Here the poverty was more appalling than I had previously witnessed. We worked our way along narrow paths winding between flimsy one-room homes built alongside open sewers. Scrawny chickens scratched the paths and scattered as we drew near. A single communal lavatory in the middle of the village filled the air with the stench of untreated sewage—so much so, I was obliged to cover my nose until I got used to it. I was grateful I had made the time, before leaving New York, to get a gamma globulin shot.

Everywhere, as if the mud had spawned them, naked babies crawled on the dirt tracks. They looked exotic with smears of medicinal black kohl around their eyes and sacred amulets, bits of colored thread, leather and beads around their wrists and ankles. In one of the doorways stood a handsome young man; he had elephantiasis, his right leg swollen to a tree-like size. Would he ever get help, or was he doomed to a painful and short life, I wondered? Often, Paulette told me, poor people in the outlying villages had no idea how to get help; their ignorance led them to accept their fate as karma.

A sick man emerged from a hut and greeted Paulette. He explained that he had had his appendix removed a few days before and had just returned from the hospital. It was obvious he had been sent home too soon and could not possibly recuperate in these conditions—open sewers, bad water and sleeping on a dirt floor beset by flies. He pulled down the old and dirty dressing around his abdomen to show us an inflamed and horrid-looking gash where the incision had been made. Paulette told him to go back to the hospital immediately, but he was too far gone and didn't have the energy. He smiled weakly and told us he would get better; he just needed some rest. Paulette put her hands on his head and said a prayer. We moved on. We stayed in the village a few hours and then returned to the city.

At the Y, wiped out by the blistering heat, I retired to my cool room for a nap. Lying on the bed in that decrepit cell, listening to the crows cawing outside, I realized I was beginning to feel a sense of belonging. My room felt familiar and friendly, and I was getting used to my bed and my mattress mates.

I was still ashamed about having been rude to Mother in the morning and felt awkward about returning to the Mother House. I went anyway and was surprised to find myself the only outsider there. Sister Henrietta said that an announcement had been made at Mass that the Mother House would be closed to outsiders in the afternoon because the sisters were having a private ceremony. I obviously had not heard it. I felt even more ashamed and apologized for intruding. I turned to leave, but Mother saw me and hustled me into the chapel, "Nonsense, nonsense, you're family."

She motioned for me to sit near the front with the novices. I had no idea what was happening until Mother began to talk about the significance of the cutting of a nun's hair. It is a symbol of each woman's detachment from the world, she explained; cutting her hair is an outward sign of her willingness to give something beautiful, something special and personal to God. After praying and singing a hymn or two, the twenty-or-so novices filed out of the chapel to relinquish their locks while the rest of us recited the Rosary. I was fascinated.

It was just three weeks after I had stopped drinking when I met Ellen. Initially, I was not at all impressed. Judging her by her appearance, she was not the type of person with whom I would ever have anything in common. She had an oval face with good cheekbones, and her Italian blood was evident in her thick black hair and her large almond-shaped eyes. Her enhancements to nature's beauty, however, were not quite as appealing—she adorned herself with yards of iridescent turquoise eye shadow that reached high into her eyebrows; she caked her long lashes with mascara and spotted her elegant cheekbones with gobs of rouge. She wore a cheap polyester skirt and blouse, hideous white sandals, and she carried an equally hideous white plastic handbag.

Then she spoke. Her voice was not vital or compelling. Something else came through—power, humor and intelligence, qualities incongruously housed in such a gaudy temple. She let slip in our conversation that she had left the convent just a few years before. A former nun! How extraordinary! How wonderful! Suddenly eye shadow, polyester and plastic fell away. I listened in awe.

Here, at last, was someone to satisfy my curiosity about the hidden lives of cloistered women, especially as she had entered the convent before the great changes of Vatican II. At last I could get answers to all the burning questions I'd had since Gumley. I was determined we would be friends.

When I met Ellen, she was working as a reservation clerk for Pan Am in their New York offices; it was her way of re-entering the world. She was amused but somewhat uncomfortable at the intensity of my interest in her. Without shame I was probing at the past she was trying to put behind her. But I thought her nun experience remarkable. I wished I were a former nun instead of a former wife. Eventually my persistent questioning broke down her resistance. She told me, as a young girl, she too had been fascinated with nuns and religious life. She had entered the convent in response to her feminine, mystical nature, which she hoped to model after

Mary. She had been disillusioned, however, to find the Church was not the spiritual path she longed for.

As our friendship grew, Ellen delighted me with her tales of convent life. Every detail of her daily routine was precisely orchestrated, even brushing her teeth. Instead of putting toothpaste on the brush like regular folk, she had to squeeze a dab into her mouth and then brush, thereby avoiding waste. She confided that although she'd changed just about everything else in her life, she still brushed her teeth the convent way. She was allowed only four pairs of underpants a year; they were darned so much that eventually there were no underpants, just darns.

I learned, too, about spiritual exercises: maintaining custody of the eyes, silence, prayer life, obedience. She told me each nun had to work on a fault a day. A good nun, she said, had to notice every time she failed in her daily routine and should focus not on the good things about herself, only on her failings. I was entranced and often exploded in gales of laughter.

We spent hours on the telephone and in coffee shops discussing drinking, relationships, sobriety and Jesus. I learned that Ellen was not only a former nun but also the daughter of a small-time Mafioso who had done time. He was in the garbage disposal business, and God only knows what or whom he really disposed. He had been inside while she was inside!

Thirty minutes passed. The novices filed back into the chapel, their heads now covered with the kerchief and veil of the Missionaries of Charity. They entered carrying their severed braids and tresses before them like sacred offerings and placed them at the foot of the statue of the Blessed Virgin in a large oval basket lined with a white cloth.

I found it a disturbing ceremony. I gazed at the novices who now looked like the rest of the sisters. This was how it was to be for them for the rest of their lives. No getting up in the morning wondering what to wear—no choice at all: just the same old outfit day after day; no more feeling the breeze blowing through their hair; no more brushing their tresses. A few of them had tears running down their cheeks, and I was keenly aware of what a sacrifice it must be. Wanting this new life with all their hearts didn't mean leaving the old one wasn't painful. The newly consecrated women passed in front of Mother, who blessed them by placing her hands on each bowed head. I got on the end of the line and let her bless me too. The ceremony had taken less than an hour. Life went on as usual, no grand celebration, no fuss, all simply part of the flow of the community's life.

I wandered around to Elliot Road to visit June. June was, as usual, most entertaining. She appeared to know everyone in Calcutta, especially Catholic priests and nuns. Her conversation was constantly punctuated with stories of Father-this, Sister-that or Brother-so-and-so. She revealed an extraordinary blend of superstition and Catholicism. "Saint Anthony finds lost articles. A quick prayer to Saint Joseph is always good for what ails you. Spilled salt must be thrown over the shoulder. Knives are never passed from one person to the next; they must be set down for the next person to pick up." She had hundreds of such precautions, antidotes and remedies.

As we sat and chatted over a cup of tea, I heard a scraping and squeaking coming from behind a curtain. June didn't say anything, but I could tell she was only pretending not to hear it. The squeaking and scraping got louder and louder until I just couldn't ignore it a moment longer.

"June, what on earth is that noise?"

With a tinge of embarrassment she replied in a rush, "Oh it's nothing, just the rat. It's so annoying. He comes every night at this time. He comes up through a drain in the kitchen and into the bedroom." Then she screamed for her servant, "*Ayah! Ayah!*"

A rat! Good God, how could she be so casual? If it was anything like the rats I saw in the streets, it was no joke. They were as big as squirrels with yellow fangs, and they looked as though they pumped iron. The *ayah* scurried out from another room in the flat. June, in her mortification, berated her in a mixture of Bengali and English, "Get him out. Ugh, horrid thing! Get him out."

The *ayah* disappeared into the kitchen, and we heard her banging the pipe with a pan to frighten away Monsieur le Rat. I got the impression, however, that all the theatrics were for my benefit and that, on a day-to-day basis, the inhabitants of Mrs. Bateman's flat lived quite amicably with her furry intruder. The squealing and scraping stopped, and June bravely steered the conversation along another path, but I was still incredulous about her tenant and wanted to know more.

"How long has he been coming? What can you do about it?" With a tut and a sigh she took me behind the curtain into the bedroom beside the kitchen, and showed me where a corner of the bed was now supported by books because the unwelcome visitor had gnawed away one of the legs.

To many residents of Calcutta, Mrs. Bateman's flat would have been the height of luxury, yet the building was old and dilapidated; water was brought in daily and hauled up the stairs by the water *wallah*; the drainage system was pretty much shot—all conditions conducive to vermin. I had seen what I thought were mice running around under the tables in Flury's, the smart café on Park Street. Maybe they were baby rats!

Saturday,
March 28, 1981

Mass over, Mother stood on the balcony as usual to greet the visitors; many tried in some way to embrace or kiss her. Eminently huggable, she invariably shifted her body or put her head down. She didn't want to be embraced or kissed. I was intrigued and wondered why.

When the visitors had left, Mother asked me to wait for her in the parlor while she had breakfast. No outsider ate with the sisters; indeed, not only the refectory but most of the Mother House was off limits to outsiders. A half curtain hanging from the tops of doorways marked the division between convent and public areas and signified the sisters' separation from the world. I sat at the square wooden table and ate the breakfast that was brought to me—a banana, bread and milky tea. On the walls was a photograph of a beaming Mother Teresa with the Pope and a large framed picture of the Sacred Heart. Covered in plastic was a hand-colored map of the world, stuck with different colored pins indicating Missionaries of Charity houses.

Mother joined me shortly (she must have wolfed down her breakfast); she was in an inquisitive mood and wanted me to explain more about alcoholism. I began by telling her that alcoholism is often referred to as "a misguided longing for the spiritual path," and my own experience seemed to confirm that belief. Throughout my drinking, although I couldn't identify it as such, I'd had an insatiable thirst, a deep yearning for God—a yearning to be filled with "the spirit." Maybe that's why I ingested such great quantities of it! Mother chuckled.

Over the years the disease of alcoholism had slowly and effectively eroded the very fabric of my life. I thought my anger and my odd behavior were due to my unhappy marriage and my frustration at work. But my marriage was over; I had become a successful auctioneer, and yet still I felt like an outsider, empty and dissatisfied. I realized I had had these same feelings for years. Other characters in my life had come and gone, but there was always one person who was featured in every disastrous episode—one person who was always at the scene of every tawdry crime. Now the evidence was clearly pointing straight to me. *I* was the common denominator. I was forced to look at myself.

I thought alcohol gave me the courage I needed, but in fact it gave me a false courage. I thought it allowed me to be honest, but the line between truth and lies blurred. I thought it enabled me to relate to others, but all it did was separate me.

I told Mother how Ellen had helped me understand I didn't need to drink. Ellen said I could renew my spirit and find my courage another way. "If you really want to," she had explained, "you can develop a quality that will enable you to walk through life as a spiritual warrior, a quiver of golden arrows slung on your back, and as you face an enemy from within or a situation that you're not sure how to handle, you will be able to reach back into your quiver, select the perfect arrow, fit it in your bow, take aim and hit the bull's eye every time." I made all the appropriate facial expressions and arm movements to emphasize the story.

It was an electrifying image, and I could see Mother thought so too.

She listened intent on trying to understand as I explained the disease concept to her. I compared it to leprosy. Alcoholics often describe themselves as social lepers; they feel ashamed, alienated, and act in ways that further alienate them from the society to which they so desperately want to belong. As the disease progresses, the alcoholic loses things— not toes and fingers as the leper does, but jobs, friends, family and eventually, his or her very life. As with leprosy, alcoholism can be arrested, but it cannot be cured.

Then Mother told me that a lot of the men I saw lying in the streets were, in fact, drunk. I was surprised; I had always thought they were the sick and the dying; in a sense they *were* the sick and the dying. "There are many addicts amongst the poor of Calcutta," she said, "alcohol is the biggest problem." She went on to tell me about *bangla*, an illegal and lethal concoction brewed by the street people. Made from sugar cane, refuse and entrails, *bangla* was fermented and hidden away from the authorities in the sewers, where it was exposed to all sorts of waste, rat droppings and God knows what else. It was poison, and anyone who drank the stuff was inviting insanity and death.

"We have had success in dealing with every kind of suffering human except the alcoholic," she said. "The sisters are perplexed by the behavior of the alcoholics they deal with. Sometimes they can be so nice and at other times rude and even violent. The sisters have no way of handling them. They give the man a blanket, and he sells it to buy more *bangla*."

I explained that I believe it is from the shared experience with another alcoholic that the healing process begins. I told her the practice of constantly making things all right for the alcoholic is called "enabling." Through bitter experience those close to the alcoholic learn not to make the situation more comfortable but to practice "tough love"—allowing the sufferer to "hit bottom."

Then to lighten the conversation, I asked, "Mother, why are you so interested in all this? Did you know one of the traits of an alcoholic is a fascination with alcohol and drinking?" I joked with her about the words **I Thirst** written in large letters next to the crucifix in the chapel. "Mother, of all the words in the Bible you could have chosen, you chose something to do with drinking."

She hurriedly interrupted me. "It is nothing at all to do with drinking. It's a reference to Christ's thirsting for souls."

I continued to tease. "Well, I don't know, Mother. I'm not convinced. Are you sure *you* don't have a drinking problem?"

She played along and, looking at me sideways, said, "Maybe." We both laughed. I wanted to hug her but held back and squeezed her hand instead.

After breakfast I collected my grey laundry from the laundry *wallah*, who squatted by the front door in the lobby of the Y, the freshly pressed clothes laid out in piles on a sheet beside him. In Calcutta, because of the dirt and the heat, I had my clothes laundered daily. There were no launderettes; the service came to me personally through George, who collected and delivered it every morning. It was an efficient, one-day service, and the clothes were returned beautifully pressed but, alas, a slightly darker shade of gray each time. For this dubious privilege, I let George charge me three rupees an item, an amount any Calcuttan would have considered outrageous.

On my way to the bazaar one afternoon, I uncovered the mystery of the dingy wash. I came upon the laundry facility; it was, in fact, a lean-to on the side of the street. In the dark interior someone was pressing the clothes with a vintage flatiron heated by coals. George was in the street gutter, on his haunches, washing the clothes in a large soapy puddle. Despite my newfound knowledge, I continued to use his service. First, no one else, apart from the smartest hotels, would launder it any differently; second, I didn't want to do it myself; third, when in Rome and all that, and fourth, it was a contribution to the local economy.

I spent the entire day at Kalighat dressing gaping bedsores—swabbing out the enormous holes and stuffing them with ointment-soaked lint. I cut hair, clipped nails, and swept the floor several times. I washed patients, fed them, cradled them and sang a few Beatles songs. Then much to everyone's amusement, I gave a rendition of "I've Been Working on the Railroad." The sisters giggled, and the old crones crooned and clapped their hands along with me.

> *I'm a little teapot, short and stout. . . .*
> *Tip me up and pour me out. . . . (spin and curtsey).*
> *I must have looked very comical doing this teapot routine, because I was plump, uninhibited, and probably looked like a teapot. My parents and their friends would roll up laughing and beg me to do it again, but I'd refuse because I could tell they were not taking me seriously. They would plead and promise they wouldn't laugh if only I'd do it just one more time. I always fell for their entreaties. I'd take a deep breath and launch into my recital. I'd barely get the first line out when they'd start again. Tears streaming down their faces, they'd howl and slap their knees. I didn't like being made fun of, but on the other hand, I loved performing and showing off.*

Working side-by-side with the sisters gave me an opportunity to share vicariously in their lives without actually crossing the convent line. The work was often tedious and usually heart-wrenching, but no task was ever rushed or performed in a casual manner. They were joyful and that joy was infectious. Even when wrapping the dead for the little tiled room, they were cheerful yet respectful. I never saw a Missionary of Charity sister pouting or complaining. "Each nun should possess a spirit of joy," was written in the Constitution of the Order. Difficult though it was for me to comprehend being consistently joyful in the face of all the "distressing disguises" of Jesus, I could not deny what I saw; the sisters' faces reflected the joy they felt within; they went about their work with boundless amounts of it. They, like Mother Teresa, were women in love.

I was as fascinated with the daily routine of the sisters as I had been with Ellen's tales of convent life. They rose every morning at four-forty and were in the chapel by five for morning prayers and meditation. At six there was Mass followed by breakfast. After breakfast, their workday began: washing was done and housework taken care of. Then the majority of sisters departed for the various schools and dispensaries. Those in "formation"—postulants studying to be novices, or novices preparing to take Vows—stayed in the house to study. At noon those who had gone out returned for lunch and a half-hour rest. By two o'clock they were off again. Usually their day was over by six, and they returned to the Mother House for Adoration, followed by tea and recreation.

Recreation obviously did not mean talking on the telephone, playing cards, smoking cigarettes, listening to music or doing their nails, but rather covering their books, writing letters, studying English, or sewing and darning. Darning saris was an art. Made of the poorest cotton, they were constantly tearing and in need of mending. It was touching to see heads bent in prayer covered with beautifully woven repairs. When a Missionaries of Charity sister mends her sari, she doesn't use cotton from a spool; instead she takes a strip of cotton material and separates a thread from it; using new thread would only tear the old garment, echoing Jesus' words about putting new wine into old skins.

A Missionaries of Charity sister has very little. Besides her devotional books, she has a tin plate and mug, three habits and three saris—two for everyday wear and one for feast days, holy days and other special occasions. She carries a rosary and a large crucifix secured by a cincture around her waist. A smaller cross is pinned to her left shoulder above the heart. Mother told me Indian women keep the keys of their homes, and therefore their treasures, next to their heart, and since a Missionaries of Charity sister considers the crucifix her treasure, she too wears it close to her heart. The only other item she has is a metal bucket with her number painted on the side. Looking at the yards and yards of saris drying on the roof, I wondered how each nun identified her own length of fabric until Paulette explained that every sister is assigned a number. The number painted on her bucket is also sewn in tiny red figures onto a corner of her sari. Paulette's was 315.

When Mother Teresa first arrived in Calcutta, India was under British rule, and Calcutta was the capital. All textbooks for school and all devotional books were written in English; hence English became the language of the Order. Communicating in one language served as a protection against the forming of ethnic groups or cliques and helped those sisters of a different culture to feel included. They were always together—they worked together, prayed together, had recreation together, traveled together and slept in dormitories. Although they embraced the spirit of community living, they told me that rarely having time alone was the hardest part of religious life.

Complete obedience kept their lives simple, and although

I was not keen on, nor did I particularly agree with, all their pre-Vatican II Catholic views, I admired their simplicity and unquestioning loyalty to the Church.

Whenever I met with Ellen, all I wanted was to talk about sobriety and Jesus and to hear her interpretation of Jesus' life. We discussed ad infinitum, *Peter, Paul and Judas. Pilate too was a favorite. We went over the Agony in the Garden, the Crucifixion and Resurrection again and again. I never tired of it. Eventually I knew I had to go and see the land where Jesus had spent his earthly life. I wanted to tread the same soil; I wanted to breathe the same air, to feel the sun on my skin, to see it rise and set over Galilee. I wanted to experience the same things he had experienced in his everyday life. I made plans to visit Israel.*

Arriving in Tel Aviv ten days after my father's memorial service, I took a bus to Jerusalem. As I looked out the window at the scrubby landscape shimmering in the heat, I kept saying over and over to myself as though I couldn't quite believe I was truly here: "This is the land that Jesus loved; this is where He walked."

As soon as I set eyes upon the walls of Jerusalem, I was caught by its allure. That the physical city Jesus knew had been destroyed in 70 AD mattered to me not at all. My first sight when I walked through the arched Jaffa Gate was flocks of sheep with their shepherds. The shepherds were carrying staffs and wore the typical Arab headdress and wool jackets over their djellabas. *It was a picture I'd seen a hundred times on Christmas cards.*

I was eager to find the Via Dolorosa along which Jesus had carried his cross—I'd walked the route so often in my mind. Thinking it would be a well-marked and obvious boulevard, I was surprised to discover I was already wandering along it. In Jerusalem, although there are many churches, there is no public statue of Jesus; He remains still somewhat hidden.

I liked this anonymity, because along those cobbled and stepped streets it was easy to imagine the ordinary yet momentous event two thousand years ago—Roman soldiers hurrying the condemned and beaten man towards Golgotha through throngs of jeering, weeping or silent bystanders and Jesus, staggering under the weight of his cross, nothing about his physical appearance setting him apart from the hundreds of other prisoners who, like him, had walked this same path from the Praetorium to the hill of execution just beyond the city walls.

To the Jews of his day, Jesus' accomplishments were mostly talk and rumor. Messiahs were two-a-penny. There were those who claimed Jesus worked miracles. What chicanery! He probably paid off a couple of beggars to claim they'd been healed. How different it all might have been if anyone had believed or understood that the sorry wretch passing before them, weighted down under his cross, was the Savior of the World, the Passover Lamb being led to slaughter.

I wonder, too, if Jesus fully understood the significance of what was happening. His earthly task seemed thwarted; his disciples were scattered. There was no heavenly host to support or save him or even to mop his brow. Where were the multitudes he'd fed and healed? His efforts must have seemed pointless, and the immediate future hideous. Or could he, even through all the pain, envision the glory of the Resurrection? There is a line by Malcolm Muggeridge I keep written in my diary: "In earthly terms, his mission was a failure."

I stayed at the Ecce Homo convent run by the Sisters of Zion. The convent was built on the site of the Roman fortress, Antonia, where Pontius Pilate tried Jesus. A section of the fortress' courtyard is still intact beneath the convent. I went down to the basement one evening and, since I was alone, slipped off my sandals and stood on the ancient flagstones where His feet, those holy feet, might have stood. Scratched into the flagstones at one end of the yard was a board game—a series of crossed lines on which the soldiers played a game using dice. It was easy to conjure up how the garrison must have been: ribald, bawdy jokes; musings about home and family; comings and goings as men changed their shifts and duties; horses groomed and brushed, their hooves clopping and echoing across the yard. Most of the rank-and-file soldiers were mercenaries from Gaul, Britain, Phoenicia, Syria and all the conquered territories of the Roman Empire.

In that same place where my bare feet were feeling the delightful coolness of the stone, they tied Jesus to a pillar and flogged him. Pilate, had ordered a token beating, but the floggers would add a little extra; it was an opportunity to vent their anger and frustration towards this hateful country and its stubborn inhabitants. The cat-of-nine-tails, a whip of leather strips studded with slivers of metal and sharpened bone, could reduce a man's back to bloody ribbons in a few strokes. Jesus got thirty-nine. It seems to be the universal nature of brutes that once they have physical power over people they sense are superior, they become even more brutal.

Observing how political prisoners have been treated throughout history, it is not difficult to imagine how Jesus fared at the hands of the soldiers. The appearance on the scene of this upstart Jew, who had been overturning tables in the Temple just a few days before, must have offered an opportunity for revenge and comic relief. There certainly wasn't much else to laugh about in this hot and hostile hole. Here before them was one of those circumcised wretches, and this one fancied himself a King, no less. "We'll show him about being a king. Here, cut me a clump of thorns; we'll crown the blighter."

In the very place I was standing, Jesus was forced to take up the rough cross on his torn and bleeding back, and, stumbling out of the courtyard, he started on his way to Golgotha. I tried to feel the vibrations through the soles of my feet. I prayed for myself and for all who brutalize. I had never picked up a whip and scourged a human or creature, but I had been cruel in other ways. I'd gossiped, been neglectful, insensitive. How many times had I hurt someone and disguised it as being truthful? How many times had I been cruel to animals or killed insects because they bothered or frightened me, not realizing how much more I must have frightened them? How many times had I ignored people or not given them my time because I had considered them to be dull or uninteresting? How could any creation of God's be uninteresting? How much had I contributed to the world's pain by my ignorance and fear? In that ancient courtyard I prayed for forgiveness and for help in my future relationship with all of God's creation.

I visited the courtyard often and meditated on the last few hours of Christ's earthly life. It was here that Pilate presented Jesus to the crowd saying, "Ecce Homo" (behold the man). Every time I get to the part of the story where Jesus is brought before Pilate, I often fantasize Pilate's saying, "I find no fault with this man; in fact I rather like him, and if anyone so much as touches a hair on his head, he'll have me to answer to."

After the day's work at Kalighat, the sisters and volunteers piled into a windowless grey truck with a big red cross painted on the back door; it was tied shut with string. The truck pulled up at the Mother House. The familiar group of beggars squatted on the pavement outside.

Sunday, March 29, 1981

The crows awakened me at the usual hour, but I was so tired, I rolled over again. When I did eventually get out of bed, I decided to take the morning off. I sat by the tennis courts under a shade tree and spent a few lazy hours writing my diary, listening to the sounds of the city and thinking about New York.

I was looking forward to being back in my apartment, engaged in my regular routine. But something beneath that desire nagged me. I couldn't give it a name. I reflected on how lucky I was to be able to spend so much time with Mother Teresa. She was everything I admired: she was loving, she was successful, she was deeply spiritual, she had a simple personal life and she traveled. I thought about my own travels, and in this meditative state the memory of my trip to Israel came back to me. Love of Jesus had put me here in India just as love of Jesus had called me to Israel.

On the last day of my stay in Jerusalem, I wanted to visit the Garden of Gethsemane. I had taken the Arab bus to a small village at the top of the Mount of Olives. The village was a huddle of a few baked mud houses; children, donkeys and a goat or two lingered outside. It was one of those mysterious, still days of brilliant blue skies and not a murmur of wind. I was acutely aware of insects humming in the grasses as I started strolling back down the hill sloping towards Jerusalem. Delightful fragrances arose from the multifarious wild flowers and herbs that flourished on the hillside. I was quite alone.

On the dusty, gravel path, I imagined myself strolling with Jesus and the Twelve as they headed towards the city having spent the night in Bethany at the home of Martha and Mary and their brother Lazarus. I was retracing the steps trod for centuries by pilgrims and merchants, prophets and soldiers, the rich, the poor, the proud, the humble.

I was looking down at the city as Jesus must have when he lamented, "O Jerusalem, Jerusalem, thou that killest the prophets, and stonest them which are sent unto thee. How often would I have gathered thy children together, even as a hen gathereth her chicks under her wings, and ye would not!" (Matt. 23:37) I could see all the sites I had seen from the roof of Ecce Homo: the whited sepulchers, the Kidron Valley, the flashing dome of the Temple Rock where Abraham prepared to slaughter his son; everywhere my eye rested, evoked a biblical scene.

I arrived at the garden just after noon. A notice on the gate stated that the Garden closed for lunch at noon and would re-open at one. I decided to wait. I selected a shady spot, and, leaning back against a rock, settled down for a quiet hour just to watch the sky and gaze at Jerusalem from this perfect vantage point. I was feeling wonderfully lazy and lulled by the tranquility of it all. Dreamily, absentmindedly, my hand reached to my neck where I wore a small gold ring on a chain.

No! No! Oh God no! In an instant I was jolted out of my serenity. The chain and ring were gone! I was on my feet. Panic gripped my stomach. The ring was a child's ring from the second century BC. It had been a gift to me, and I had had it only a few weeks. Because it was so small, and wouldn't fit on any of my fingers, I put it on a chain around my neck. Now it was gone! I felt sick.

A year before, I had traveled to New Hampshire to visit the Evanses. They were good New England stock—hardy and tweedy. Mrs. Evans was the sort of woman I imagined as American pioneer. She baked beautifully, preserved fruit, knitted socks, quilted, wore sensible shoes. Mr. Evans was a collector of Japanese art. I had made the trip to select pieces for a future auction. He also had a modest, but extremely fine, collection of Roman jewelry; he was delighted when I expressed an interest and took great pleasure in showing it to me.

As I had pored over the trays of brooches, arm-bands, necklaces and earrings, my eye had been caught by a simple, exquisitely wrought child's ring of rich, yellow gold set with a carnelian intaglio. Mr. Evans told me its history and how he came to acquire it. Eight months later, and just a few weeks before my father died, I returned to New Hampshire. During the long drive I was thinking about my previous visit and how much I liked being around the Evanses. I recalled Mr. Evans' Roman jewelry collection and mused that if I ever had the money, I'd buy a ring like that child's ring. It was a fleeting thought.

Shortly after I arrived, dinner was served. On my plate was a small envelope with my name on it. Puzzled, I opened it. Inside was the ring! The very ring I had been thinking about! I was flabbergasted. It was so generous and unexpected. This magnificent piece was now mine. I wasn't quite sure exactly why the Evanses had given it to me, but I didn't question it. I was ecstatic. I could feel God's hand in the whole affair. I felt it was a sign of His closeness to me, of His involvement in every aspect of my life, of His awareness of all my desires, no matter how passing or materialistic. I treasured the knowledge and the ring.

Now I'd lost my treasure. In my anguish I thought of retracing my steps but knew a search would be futile. I wasn't at all sure when or where it had fallen, and it was so small, it would just have blended into the yellow gravel. Or I could have dropped it on the bus, or in the village, or in the café I'd stopped in. I was devastated. The ring *had been prized for over two thousand years, and now, clumsily, I'd lost it. I couldn't be trusted with anything. Why hadn't I bought a better chain? It shouldn't have been on a chain around my neck in the first place; I was stupid to wear it. I should have kept it in a box as the Evanses had.*

I was well into the process of self-flagellation when suddenly a new thought came to me, "What on earth are you so het up about? God gave you the ring. All you supplied was a tiny desire. If it's the baubles of the world you want, you can have them. But why not step higher? Why not seek life's real treasures? Treasures that will last forever—treasures that can never be lost or taken away. Treasures that will enrich your life and the lives of others—the gifts of the Holy Spirit: peace, understanding, love, wisdom, compassion, courage. Why not seek those things?

In retrospect I know it was not my thought. The panic in my stomach about the lost ring subsided. Yes, of course I wanted the gifts of the Holy Spirit. I was excited by the prospect of filling my spiritual quiver with those same qualities Jesus embodied. But what on earth was I supposed to do? My inner voice spoke again, "Just do the next thing in front of you and rely on me. I will do the rest." This was just what Ellen was always telling me.

On the Mount of Olives, in the very spot where Jesus had agonized about saying "Yes" to the next step, I said "Yes" and with that "Yes" I began another phase of my journey. I felt a deep gratitude for my life; I was sober and now had a yearning for something higher.

If I had known then anything about the way God shapes those who seek Him, I might not have been so eager. I had some notion that attributes like tolerance were simply bestowed. I was to learn differently. God does not just shower tolerance down from on high. What God does bestow is many irritating people and situations so one might learn the lesson. Tolerance and patience have been my hardest lessons. I still find myself annoyed with people who talk during a

movie, people who don't rush in rush hour. I don't understand why
people fiddle about or procrastinate. I want to lose ten pounds and
lose it now. I could go on about what irritates me, but it's got very
little to do with the circumstances. It's the way I keep reacting and
reacting. I'm also mortified when I'm reminded that intolerance is
ignorance manifested.

I didn't know it then, and still find it difficult to understand that
God has already given me everything I need. It's just that I have
covered my tolerance with intolerance, my compassion with pity,
my courage with fear and my tenderness with rigidity. I have also
found I have an inclination to clutch rhinestones to my breast while
God is waiting to give me diamonds. Mother once wrote to me, "The
only true thing I can offer God is my emptiness; even God cannot fill
that which is full."

The more I thought of my path and the lessons I had
learned, the more I understood how great was Mother Teresa's
love. Yes, I thought, she is a saint; she has the qualities and
foibles often attributed to saints. She can be impatient; she
does not tolerate fools easily, yet she has great compassion.
She keeps her eye on the details as well as the big picture. She
never answers an enquiry with deep theological answers but
with disarming simplicity. She's soft and pliable in responding
to the urgings of the Holy Spirit, and her conviction and faith
are unshakable.

In one way or another, I believe all are called to do
what Mother Teresa does—to be loving and to serve humanity
in our daily lives in whatever form it might take: pastry cook,
messiah, mechanic, emperor, housewife, poet, executive,
saint, ballet dancer. So few of us ever step up to the plate, that
when one of us does, it appears extraordinary. When told
she was extraordinary, Mother usually responded, "There
are many people God could have chosen to do this work.

I cannot know why He chose me, but I accept His will unquestioningly, and you should do the same. It will bring you great joy."

That Mother enjoyed my company played on my ego. It was tempting to remain here, to be with this woman who accepted me, to follow her, to have a life centered upon serving God, to have my wardrobe taken care of once and for all, to escape worry about rent, money, love affairs. Community life had always looked tempting, especially this order of nuns, yet I knew in my heart this was not a genuine calling. When God calls, it's a call to serve Him, not to follow someone else, no matter how wonderful that person might be, no matter how good or holy. And besides, I took myself with me wherever I went—whether in a corporate setting or a convent.

I spent the afternoon at Kalighat. I busied myself once again at my self appointed task of cutting finger and toe nails and washing feet. Repulsive though it was, I rather enjoyed the work. Jesus had washed the feet of the disciples, whose feet, I am sure, were just as neglected as the feet at Kalighat.

The sunset was glorious; the city's heavy pollution served to intensify the purples and oranges in the evening sky. After supper, I decided to stop by June's. She was as welcoming as always. At around nine o'clock there was a knock on the door. June got up and fetched a bedroll and blanket, opened the door, handed them out with a breezy "Good night, Mr. Collins," and shut the door again. Mr. Collins used to be a schoolteacher but had fallen on hard times, so she let him sleep on her landing. "He's a bit of a scoundrel," she said, "but even scoundrels need help and a place to sleep."

When I left I had to step over the sleeping Mr. Collins.

Monday,
March 30, 1981

When I came creeping downstairs at the Y at four-thirty in the morning, the porter was ready for me. He was no more delighted about being disturbed at that early hour than he had been my first morning, but a few rupees in his palm had eased his discomfort.

Early morning was the only time the city was relatively quiet and spacious—a state which lasted for a short, blissful span before the multitudes emerged and the racket began anew. The morning routine seemed familiar to me now; even the enormous rats with their yellow teeth were beginning to feel like family. I watched them scurry furtively along the sides of the buildings and disappear through cracks or down drains. Along Rippon Street, I passed a group of men who, after Mother's enlightening talk, I realized were probably drunks. They were slumped against a wall, sleeping with the stray dogs.

Dogs were an integral part of Calcutta life and were treated with disguised affection. During the day they were cursed, kicked and shooed off, but at night one saw the street orphans curl up with these pitiful creatures for mutual warmth. June told me that at one time city officials had devised a plan to round up all stray dogs and have them put down. But suddenly every scabby cur acquired an owner— shopkeepers and street dwellers "adopted" dogs, and not one mangy mongrel was taken into custody or destroyed.

I arrived at Mass wearing olive green slacks and a matching shirt I had purchased for almost nothing in a bazaar; I looked a bit like an Israeli *sabra* (female soldier). Mother took one look at me and said, "You should wear a dress. A dress is nicer. You look better in a dress."

I didn't go berserk as I had over the nail polish. I said if it made her happy, I'd be more than willing to wear a dress in future. I could tell Mother was in a shaping-up mood. The next thing she wanted to know was if I went to Confession regularly.

Had anyone else asked, I would have told them it was none of their business, but with Mother, I felt it *was* her business simply because she made it so. I told her I hadn't been to Confession in fifteen years. In fact Calcutta was the first experience in my adult life of attending daily Mass. She was off! She expounded on the spiritual benefits of Confession, none of which made much sense to me, except I did know confiding one's misdeeds and faults to another could be a healing experience. Mother wanted to know if I would be willing to go to Confession there at the Mother House. The notion wasn't too appealing, but since it was Mother Teresa making the offer, how could I refuse? I put aside my pride and said, "Yes," and added I would do it when the priest came to hear the sisters' confession over the weekend. She was pleased.

Later British Airways called saying the Friday flight was full so they had booked me on a flight leaving Calcutta the following Monday. I was supposed to be back in the office Monday. Oh, well, I'd just have to cable Lucille and let her know I was going to be a few days late. It also meant I would be able to spend only one night with my mother in London before going on to New York. I was surprised how serenely I accepted this news. I certainly had changed my attitude since my visit to the ticket office the week before; God clearly wanted me to stay around a little longer.

At Prem Dan many of the patients were already outside, sitting on the low brick walls or wandering aimlessly about the yard. On the path was an odd-shaped lump completely covered in a brightly checkered cloth; it was a male patient who had decided to plonk himself down in the center of the main walkway. He was obviously squatting with his knees up around his ears so that he looked like an enormous crumpled spider under a tablecloth. No one moved him or told him he was in the way, and he stayed there for at least an hour before deciding to go inside.

I went to see Meeta. She was remarkably improved; there were now many patches of scabs forming over the burns, and just a few areas required dressings. She had become Sister Veronica's pet charge.

Paulette saw me from her office window and beckoned. I was glad to see her. She had planned to do all sorts of things, but we got chatting, and she didn't do a stroke of work. Her great love, she told me, had always been the family. When she entered the Missionaries of Charity, she found there was a need to teach natural family planning to the poor. The alternative to this was government-ordered sterilization. She had me rolling with laughter at some of her stories about starting the program, including the difficulty she had had getting pictures of genitalia drawn for teaching aids—not an easy task for any woman in India, let alone a sister. Even within the Order, she told me with a certain amount of glee, very few knew or understood exactly what she was doing, and she was considered a bit of an oddball.

I found myself slipping into the bad habit of comparing my life with hers. We were the same age, born a few days apart, but at the age of eighteen we had made very different choices. It seemed Paulette's life had been richer and more meaningful than mine. Although I recognized I had always had a pull towards the spiritual, I had not pursued that path; instead I had focused on misplaced emotional gratification, personal ambition and life's luxuries. Paulette, on the other hand, had entered the convent and focused her attention on God and the life of the spirit.

I was envious of her calling, envious of her devotion and commitment and even of her struggles to confine her spirited, iconoclastic personality within the constraints of religious life. Although at times she found life within the Missionaries of Charity restricting, even rigid, she had no doubts about her vocation. She never doubted for a moment she had made the right choice in becoming a nun; she had no regrets. On the other hand, my life had been full of regrets. It was not easy for me then to understand that my path had been right and necessary for me and that God had called me in a different way.

I wore a dress to Adoration—a pale-blue, gauzy dress with a rounded neck and full skirt. I looked positively virginal. Mother was delighted and told me how pretty I looked. It made me happy to please her. After Adoration she came to me very excitedly, her eyes flashing and crinkling. She said a priest was present and would hear my confession right away. She then gave me a pamphlet to read about Confession and said as soon as I'd finished, I should go into the room off the chapel where the priest was waiting for me.

I thought it all a bit rushed; we had only discussed it that morning. I had hoped to have at least four days to think about it, and I wasn't even sure I wanted to do this Confession thing at all. I knew I would be doing it only to please Mother but told myself it didn't really matter *why*, I should just go ahead and trust in God's providence.

I went into the sacristy. Seated on one side of the wood-framed confessional was a priest I hadn't seen before; his face was partially obscured by a tightly woven cane screen. I knelt on the unpadded kneeler and was amazed at my automatic recollection of childhood indoctrination, "Forgive me, Father, for I have sinned. It's been fifteen years since my last confession."

A chilly silence came at me from the other side of the confessional, but I ploughed ahead, desperately trying to list all my so-called sins. I couldn't possibly cover fifteen years, so I just supplied a few hastily recalled highlights. The priest kept interrupting me and asking for clarification. At one point he zeroed in on my marriage and wanted to know all the specifics of our sex life—whether or not we had used contraception. This was too much. I thought him a little too interested, perversely so. The condition of my soul, I told him, should be of more concern than the intimacies of my sex life of five years ago. I wanted to get this awful Confession business over with as soon as possible; besides my knees were killing me. He mumbled something and gave me absolution.

When I emerged, Mother was waiting for me, thrilled to bits.

I did not have the heart to tell her I thought the priest a pervert. She pulled me into the chapel. We sank to our knees, and she prayed with me. Then she took a rosary from the cord around her waist, kissed it and gave it to me. I put aside my feelings about the priest and the confession and basked in Mother's love.

Tuesday,
March 31, 1981

Today Brother Christos was taking leper patients who required surgery to Shanti Nagar, about two hundred miles northwest of Calcutta. I'd leapt at the opportunity to go; I had heard so much about this community from Paulette and was keen to visit. Besides, it was an opportunity to get out of Calcutta and see the countryside. I told Mother the day's plans, and after Mass she insisted we wait while the sisters prepared packages of fruit, sweets, prayer books and yards of white cotton for the sisters at Shanti Nagar. We picked up bananas and yogurt and went directly to the station to catch the train.

At Titagarh the brothers were preparing for our journey. Lepers, food and bottles of water were being loaded into the ambulance. As I watched the driver and his barefoot, half-naked sidekick fiddling about under the hood, I had a flash that everything was not in Divine Right Order with the engine. I pushed the thought aside.

While preparations were underway, Blondine and I wandered off beside the railway line. We were strolling and nattering when I noticed several people on the other side of the double tracks jumping up and down and gesticulating at us. I might have thought little of it since it was not unusual for us to be stared at. Suddenly, however, instinct told me something was wrong. I swung around in time to see a train flying along the tracks bearing down on us. With only seconds to spare, I hurled us out of the way. We had inadvertently strolled onto the tracks. The ground here was all the same level; there were no barriers, no signposts, no clanging bells or gates; the train had been sounding its horn, but the wind had torn the sound away so that it was indistinguishable from the regular traffic noise. Realizing Death had passed by so closely, my whole body started to shake; I held Blondine and cried uncontrollably. Thus began our journey.

We had with us six lepers, five adults and a twelve-year-old girl, Krishna, who was to have part of her foot amputated. Krishna was a solemn-faced child, and try as we might to get her to talk, she stayed very quiet, refusing even a smile. She was probably terrified of us, the strange white ladies speaking in a strange tongue. I thought it best to leave her alone. Brother Christos explained that she came from a small village and that when it was discovered she had leprosy, the villagers assembled to discuss what was to be done with her. Convinced her leprosy was a sign that some evil had befallen their village, it was decided the child should be buried alive to atone for the wrong and to appease whichever god had been offended.

Brother Christos told us that girls are not nearly as valued as boys. Indeed in some rural areas it was not unheard of for them to be drowned at birth. If Krishna had been a boy, she might not have been so expendable. In an extraordinary move to save her, Krishna's father had fled the village and carried her for days on his back to the nearest mission center; from there she had been transferred to the brothers at Titigarh. When Brother Christos had finished this tale, we were all very quiet for a while.

Besides Krishna, there were four male lepers and another

female leper, all requiring surgery to their feet, hands or face. Lepers lose sensation in their noses, fingers, toes, and eventually, their hands and feet. They become the victims of accidents—they may step on a nail, a glass shard or something hot, and, unable to feel the flesh tear or burn, the wound remains untreated. Infection sets in, and often the infected area has to be cut away so the entire limb doesn't rot.

The journey to Shanti Nagar was the most preposterous part of the trip. We traveled in what the brothers, in a wild leap of imagination and not a little faith, called an ambulance. The only resemblance to an ambulance I could see was the red cross painted on both sides of it. It was really an old battered truck. It roared like an angry beast and was obviously built before anyone had heard of suspension. It had two rows of seats in front—enough room for a driver and five passengers; the back was an empty space covered with layers of sacking to accommodate the reclining patients. To my horror I saw cockroaches the size of battleships skittering in and out of the sacking.

The driver had a picture of the baby Jesus on the sun visor above his head. He must have believed the picture offered him divine protection from calamity, because he drove like a man possessed, tossing us from side to side like sacks of turnips as he zoomed along overtaking everything in sight. His sidekick, a boy baked black by the sun, was prone on the roof acting as pilot, directing the driver around narrow curves, banging on the cab roof to transmit signals to him and yelling at everyone and everything, moving or stationery, to get out of the way. Every so often he would slither forward and peer at us, upside-down, through the top of the windshield. When the roads were clear, he would slide off the roof and stand on the running board to chat with the driver as we sped along.

The frenzied pace never slackened for a moment. It was futile to try to observe the countryside as it whizzed and bumped by. It was a blur, moving film without sprockets. Nothing registered and, to be truthful, I shut my eyes a lot. We barreled through villages, flocks of geese, oxen, people. Half the time I was shrieking, and the rest of the time I had my head buried in my hands. My heart must have stopped at least a dozen times. I didn't know which was worse—the near miss by the train earlier or riding with this madman.

Through it all Brother Christos was perfectly calm, as though he were out for a Sunday trot in the old country brougham. He was used to it, I supposed. It appeared everyone on the road was driving the same way. After a couple of hours of this intolerable abuse, the poor old engine, with a long, defeated whine, gave up. The heat and pace were too much for it.

We all piled out of the truck onto a grassy embankment. What a relief! The earth and spiky grass felt so good and still. Normally, I would have become quite agitated with this hitch in our plans, but today I was resigned. There was nothing I could do even if I had wanted to. Anyway, I found it an amusing predicament, a breakdown on an Indian highway with six lepers. What did it matter in the grand scheme of things?

I lay on my back on the grass, staring into the heavens' blue where a big, solitary cloud took its time crossing the sky.

The garden where I grew up was another of my favorite childhood places, especially in the summer. It had wide flower beds, planted in planned abundant disarray, with blooms typical of an English garden: roses, marigolds, pansies, hollyhocks, snapdragons, iris, each beauty vying for attention and shamelessly flaunting its finery. The flowerbeds bordered a lawn my father kept trim with a manual lawnmower; the green grass confetti, and the severed heads of daisies and buttercups, shot into the bin of the machine as he pushed it up and down the length of the garden, leaving formal stripes on the soft carpet. In the middle of the garden was a dip, where the lawn fell away into a hollow about fifteen feet in diameter and three and a half feet deep. We filled it with water in the hot weather and swam all day. Having a swimming pool in an English garden was quite a luxury.

Some of my fondest memories are of lying on my tummy watching the ants and other insects crawling in and out of sight among the blades, or of lying on my back, gazing at the clouds and wondering how far up Heaven was. Yellow-and-black butterflies bobbed softly around my head, and chubby bees, their leggings filled with yellow powder, bumbled from flower to flower.

The driver opened the hood of the ambulance, and a great cloud of steam arose. He and the sidekick busied themselves with the unhappy, sputtering and hissing engine. The driver unwound the rag he wore around his head and dove under the hood to wipe and clean various bits and pieces, as though cleaning the poor old thing alone would make everything all right. I don't think it even occurred to him that our speed and his wild driving might have been the cause of our dilemma. When he was done with his rubbing and wiping, he circled his head again with the greasy strip and, emitting a long yawn, settled down beside his cooling motor to take a nap. Brother Christos moved up the road and urinated. I noticed my surprise. In some holdover from childhood, I thought that when men and women dedicated themselves to God, they became exempt from bodily functions.

Forty-five minutes later the engine had cooled down; we bundled back into the vehicle and continued our journey.

Several breakdowns and a food stop later, we rolled into Shanti Nagar. It was already dark. Sister Francis Xavier, the Superior, greeted us. The lepers were taken away to the hospital, and I was happy to see Krishna being carried and coddled by two sisters. Brother Christos stayed in the cottage with the resident priest, who was also a doctor. The driver and his sidekick slept inside the ambulance. The rest of us were given a light supper and shown to a dormitory with old-fashioned iron beds draped with mosquito netting. I soon sank into blissful slumber.

Wednesday,
April 1, 1981

I felt ragged; the journey the day before had taken its toll. I was far from the well-groomed sophisticate who had arrived in Calcutta almost three weeks before. My face had been exposed to too much sun, grime and wind. My hair was dry, my nails and nail polish chipped, my feet callused, cracked and dirty.

Brother Christos celebrated Mass in a tiny, airy chapel with the now familiar **I Thirst** next to the crucifix on the wall. I read the lesson, and Brother Christos gave an inspirational homily on denial. He used the example of a leper who refused to accept that he was ill and in need of medical help. Living in a state of denial, the disease claimed more and more of his body, so by the time he finally admitted his situation, irreparable damage had occurred.

"It is the same with all of us," Brother Christos said. "Many times we cannot admit we are spiritually sick and need help. We think a new job will fix us, or a different partner, or new clothes, but what we really need is God." He also talked about how we need each other, about how we are really one big family, and about however difficult it is to love our brothers and sisters all the time, just *trying* to love them is in itself rewarding. We sat on the bare floor listening to him and then watched as he performed the rituals of the Mass with a concentration that was intimate and sacred.

Based upon yesterday's travel experience, we allowed plenty of time for the return to Calcutta. The original plan had been to arrive at Shanti Nagar after lunch and to spend the afternoon and evening with the sisters, but because of our vehicular mishaps and subsequent late arrival, we were limited to a short morning tour.

Sister Francis Xavier was, I guessed, in her late sixties, wiry-framed and animated. She, like Brother Christos, was a fully qualified doctor specializing in leprosy. They knew each other well and had a lot to talk about. In spite of the heat, she wore a shawl; I wondered if she were ill. She displayed no outward signs of ill health; quite the contrary, as she showed us around the center, she hardly stopped talking and seemed happy to have visitors. She had been at Shanti Nagar since the late 1950's and had watched it grow from a bare piece of land to the village and community it is today where lepers and their families are able to live a normal life.

We walked along well-maintained brick paths past clusters of cottages nestling under shady trees, their flower and vegetable gardens edged with neat hedges. There was, besides the modest housing, a school, a recreation center and a clean, efficient hospital.

We were sorry to have to leave so soon. Sister Xavier gave us letters for Mother and the sisters in Calcutta, and with many heartfelt exclamations of "good-bye" and "thank you" and "please pray for us," we set off.

The journey home took less time. We were taking back with us other lepers who had recovered from surgery and were returning to Titigarh. Once again we were subjected to maniacal driving but this time suffered only a couple of minor breakdowns.

I had hitherto kept my distance from the patients, but by the end of the afternoon I was so tired I thought, "Oh, what the hell!" and clambered into the back of the ambulance to lie down with them. I was too exhausted to be bothered by anything, least of all the idea of jostling around with leprosy patients on smelly sacking (shared with herculean roaches) in the back of an old battered truck.

Thursday, April 2, 1981

This morning I saw a merchant, perched like a fowl in his matchbox size shop, give a coin to a beggar. Every day I am moved by the small courtesies the people of the city offer each other. On the crowded buses, in spite of women's place in most of Indian society, I am always struck when I see a man yield his seat to a woman. No matter how tightly jammed the bus is or how fast it is traveling, this exchange is accomplished.

This morning at Kalighat a young woman was brought in. No more than fifteen or sixteen years old, she was wearing a filthy torn blouse and sari. Her ears were split where her earrings had been torn out. I had no idea what was wrong with her, but she was certainly sick; her eyes were glazed over and she could barely lift her head. What horrors had this poor girl been through on the hard streets?

Sister Luke asked if I would bathe her and cut off her hair since she had lice. Lest the place become infested, men and women who came to Kalighat with lice immediately had their hair cut short. It was procedure. This girl's hair, braided, hung below her buttocks and had probably never been cut. I shrank from the task. I pleaded with Sister Luke to let me wash it and pick out the lice; cutting it off seemed horribly extreme.

"No." Sister Luke, fortified by practicality, was adamant.

She understood my reluctance and said with a gentle firmness that if I thought it might be too difficult a task for me, she would ask someone else to do it. Yes, I felt it would indeed be difficult, but I didn't want to abandon my young charge.

I sat on the edge of the cot with the feeble girl leaning against me. I took a deep breath; silently begging her understanding and forgiveness, I began to cut. I couldn't stop my tears; she was not a stranger, she was a part of me. Maybe I was comparing my privileged Madison Avenue life with the life of this girl, too ill to protest, her hair now severed and lying, a black heap, in my lap.

On the way home I could not stop thinking about her. I was learning so much about myself through the people I was tending. They had so much less than I. Or did they?

After lunch June took me shopping in New Market, a sprawling covered market housing hundreds of vendors. Near the market we were confronted with a sight more wretched than anything I could ever have imagined, for coming towards us was a human ball—a man so hideously deformed, his arms and legs so grotesquely twisted and misshapen, I couldn't tell where they began or ended or which way they faced. Naked but for a flimsy loincloth, he was rolling himself over and over, chanting a prayer and pushing a tin plate of coins with his chin. I stood aghast at the sight of this human being rolling along in the muck and dirt of the street—cars, bicycles, rickshaws, all passing perilously close, some swerving to avoid him.

June, who had seen him many times before and was quite used to this sight, became cross. She tutted impatiently that he was in our way, and said, "Oh goodness gracious, he's so manipulative; he could crawl, but he prefers to roll. He makes more money that way."

Momentarily stunned by her reaction, my response was to burst out laughing. What did it matter if he made more money? What did it matter if he made five thousand rupees a day? His lot in life was still pitiful. But at that moment June saw him only as a pushy businessman.

At the market entrance more beggars harassed us; June pushed firmly through the beseeching crowd. I was uncomfortable. What to do about the beggars? Being a foreigner, I was constantly accosted by them; it was hard not to give, but I had been advised by the sisters on my first day, and by the other volunteers, that to give in public was unwise. I sometimes went against the advice and would find myself in a forest of outstretched hands, all desperately clutching at me. I learned how to distribute money in other ways: tipping generously, not taking the change when I bought a cup of tea on the sidewalk, tipping the workers at the Y, and I was certainly supporting George the laundry *wallah*.

Friday,
April 3, 1981

Last Monday three people were killed by the police during a riot that started when workers crossed a picket line. Because of the killings, a general strike was called for today. Fearing the streets would be dangerous, the sisters advised the volunteers not to go out. I was quite happy to oblige; it meant I could spend time with Mother, who was in a social vein.

Once again she maneuvered the conversation to the subject of alcoholism and wanted to know if it was hard for me to be around alcohol. I thought it an insightful question since often people find it difficult to understand how an alcoholic can still want to drink after years of sobriety. A common misconception is that once the alcoholic stops drinking, alcoholism "goes away" like the flu or something. I said I had to be vigilant especially around food. In restaurants I always check to make sure the food is not cooked in alcohol of some sort. "I cannot tease the disease." I told her. "It's like tickling the neck of a tiger. For a long time the tiger may purr, but a tiger is not pussycat, and one day it might not feel like purring and with one good swat rip me apart. And around alcohol in any form, I'm like a vampire around blood; I can sniff it out, and it sets off a craving. If I am not vigilant, over time my guard can be lowered, and I have thoughts of 'I have this thing mastered,' or 'I am in control.' I am deluded into feeling powerful instead of powerless, but I've learned to have respect for tigers as well as alcohol and to keep a safe distance from them both."

I told her I sometimes found Mass at the Mother House a little uncomfortable, especially on those days when the priest dips the host in the wine. I always have to stop him mid-dip to say I only want the host. It would be easy for me to justify having the wine by saying, "This isn't wine; this is the blood of Jesus." Mother responded by saying that if I felt uncomfortable, I should go to the other side of the chapel during Communion where she distributed the plain host to the sisters.

"That's not the point," I said, "it's important I claim what I know to be right for me even if I am embarrassed." I told her that many times I was tempted not to even take Communion in order to avoid the rigmarole and awkwardness of having to say "no wine" with people waiting in the line behind me. But at those times I would think of the tremendous gift I'd been given, and the thought inspired me to hold fast.

The strike broke down in the afternoon, and city life moved again. We were relieved since one of the English volunteers was going to Bombay by train, and a few of us wanted to see her off. We bundled into a taxi. It took the usual perilous ride through the maze and congestion of Calcutta, over the Howrah Bridge, and deposited us outside the enormous, red-brick Victorian edifice of Howrah Station.

Howrah Station makes Grand Central at rush hour appear positively bucolic. As the trains pull into the station, they transmogrify into a river of humanity pouring out of the carriages. Carriages designed to accommodate four hundred people expel over a thousand. To try to go against the flow of this organic mass would be to manifest a death wish.

The river of bodies pours down the platforms and spills like Niagara over the steps of the station entrance and divides into the tributaries of the Calcutta streets. Villagers arrive at all hours with enormous baskets of vegetables balanced upon their heads and babies in their arms; I saw some with the flopping tails of large fish poking out of their packages. Even before the hordes arrive, the platforms are already congested with vendors selling edibles—baskets of bananas, oranges or spicy crunchy-munchies. Through them the newly arrived masses stream by, surprisingly seldom bumping or tripping over each other.

Running bare-footed amidst the flow are the porters wearing red shirts and the customary khaki shorts, stacks of suitcases piled on their heads. Looking at their stick-like legs moving so rapidly beneath them, I was surprised the heavy loads didn't just drill them into the ground like human screws. They take the luggage from a passenger and, never once glancing back, sprint down the length of the platform and through the station to the waiting taxis. I marveled how, in all that teeming humanity, customers and porters recognized and found each other again.

Howrah Station was also home to many of the street urchins. The main concourse was like the heart of a beehive, and amidst the constant to-ing and fro-ing were groups of raggedy children, seven-year-olds taking care of four-year-olds. Some were asleep, huddled together right in the middle of the floor. No one moved them; everyone adjusted and walked around them. By the age of seven they were already skilled at stealing and pick-pocketing. They were controlled by pimps or *gundas* (crooks)—India's 20th century version of Fagin in Dickens' *Oliver Twist*.

Saturday,
April 4, 1981

This morning, when it came time to distribute Communion, I saw Mother switch places with the priest and stand on my side of the chapel. I knew her gesture was in response to our conversation about the communion wine. Such a profound kindness enfolded in silence and hidden from public gaze, her exquisite sensitivity gave me an awareness of being truly enveloped in the Everlasting Arms.

Back to Prem Dan again. I went with Paulette to visit more villages. It was a hurried morning, but we were able to chat on the train ride home. I told her how much I loved talking with Mother. Paulette said, "Mother really loves you. She thinks you're very special." My eyes filled with tears; my relationship with my own mother was still such an enigma to me.

My maternal grandmother had been a remote, undemonstrative woman who taught my mother to be distant. I remember once being surprised when my mother showed concern for me in a way I could understand: I was returning from school hours late and walking home from the train station, I saw her coming toward me. She was obviously distraught but said very little. I think she must have made a promise to God that if He delivered me home safely, she would be content and not reprimand or punish me. I was never late from

*school again. Even though my visit with her on the way to India had
been difficult, I was looking forward to seeing her again.*

I went to Kalighat in the afternoon for the last time. Now
I was able to sit with the patients and take the time to feed
each one carefully. I remembered how difficult this task had
been on my first day. Now I was able to stroke their faces and
cradle their cropped heads against my chest while I spooned
food between cracked lips. As if they were babies, I happily
and patiently spoon-fed these frail bodies of Christ.

Sunday,
April 5, 1981

My last full day in Calcutta. I had agreed to go with Paulette to the Howrah district, where she taught Sunday school to a group of teenage boys. Before we left, she served me breakfast in the parlor: bread, tea and a pale-yoked egg swimming in a puddle of grease. I knew not to waste Missionaries of Charity food, so I gulped down the slimy thing trying not to think about it too much.

Although it was Sunday, the streets were just as congested as they were on weekdays. We attended Mass in a large church near Howrah station before going to the adjacent schoolhouse where Paulette's boys were gathered. This morning there was no Bible study or catechism. Instead, I was to be the lesson. Paulette told the group I was visiting from America. They were in awe; they had never seen or spoken to an American before. Although they were in their teens, they seemed younger and more innocent than American youth, and yet they probably had seen and experienced more of life than most of their Western counterparts. They were eager to know everything about the States and pumped me with questions about myself, about movie stars, about space travel and about big houses. They had the impression everyone in America was rich— in many ways it was true. They were astonished to learn I had no servants and no car; it didn't match their image of life in the USA. I felt a little sorry for having shattered the myth.

Sadness fell like a shadow between Paulette and me. I had wanted so much to leave Calcutta in the beginning, but now, with my departure imminent, I wasn't so certain. Meeting Mother, Paulette, and the Missionaries of Charity was like coming up against a high wall and clambering up it to peer over the top. What I saw on the other side was a life of freedom through the spirit; it filled me with hope and excitement; it was a place I wanted to be. But I did not have the strength to pull myself up and over the wall, and I had to drop back down to my side. It troubled me. Now I'd seen this other dimension, I had an inkling the life I was returning to would no longer hold the charm it once had.

On the way back in the bus, Paulette asked me to tell her about the Holy Land. She said she wanted to go there but doubted she'd ever have an opportunity. So I told her about Jerusalem, about the convent I had stayed in, about standing on the flagstones. I told her about the Mount of Olives and how the light looked in Israel. I recalled Galilee and told her how one evening, as I was strolling along the quayside, I had an irresistible urge to immerse myself in the lake, to be held by the body of water that had embraced Christ so many times. "There was no one around, so I slipped off my sandals and jumped in fully clothed."

Paulette's eyes widened with glee and approval. She clapped her hands exultantly. It appealed to her as it had me. Something about the act was enthralling—baptism in the holy waters. Whether prankish or holy, I wasn't sure.

I emerged minutes later; I might have stayed longer but feared someone would happen along. Naturally, my linen dress was sopping, but I knew it wouldn't take long to dry since, even though the sun had set, it was still hot.

As I walked back to the hostel, I passed the Scottish Christian chapel where a service was in progress, and, eager not to miss a thing, I joined the small congregation. Fortunately my dress was black so one couldn't tell it was soaking. When the service was over, on the wooden pew was a sizable puddle I thought prudent to leave unattended and unexplained.

Paulette was beside herself laughing and prodded me to tell her more. I told her about reading the Bible for the first time, how I experienced another awakening.

I had read many books about Jesus, I told her. But for some reason I had avoided the biblical account of his life. I don't know why; perhaps I thought it would be too heavy-going. And growing up Catholic in the 'fifties, we learned our catechism and read about the lives of the saints, but the Bible was not a part of our education. Now I wanted to read it and, being in the Holy Land, thought I couldn't have been in a more ideal place to make a start.

I found a small, red, plastic-covered King James version of the New Testament in a souvenir shop, and every day I sat by the lake and read it. After plodding through the first eighteen verses of Matthew with the endless list of fathers and sons whose names I couldn't pronounce, it was as though something held my eyes and fastened them on the page. All the stories and snippets I had from various sources were woven together in a fascinating continuum. The life of Jesus blossomed for me—His words, His deeds, His struggles. I could not put the book down.

During the few days it took me to read the New Testament, the Proverbs and Psalms, I felt my heart opening. It was three weeks since my father's death, and my heart was already in a softer, more open state. Time and again tears spilled down my cheeks; I was able to mourn his death, to feel some long-sealed door had gently opened, and like fish spilling from an over-filled net, my feelings tumbled out. I don't know how long I sat in that state, reflecting, mourning, joyful, hopeful, free. It had been very simple, very quiet; the still, clear voice had spoken from an inexpensive, plastic-covered bible. Life was going on around me: the sun was shining; boats were bobbing on the lake; my feet were dangling in the water. Nothing had changed in the world, and yet for me, the whole world had shifted.

Several times I have experienced this sudden, almost ordinary sense of seeing the world around me differently. It is like standing for years with one's back to a mountain vista and then turning around to see the incredible magnificence that was there all along.

I told Paulette what an impact *she* had had on me and how fortunate I felt to have such wonderful teachers in my life. I told her about Ellen. I recounted how Ellen would say, "I cannot teach you anything that on some level you don't already know. It's all within you." I also told her that Ellen had pointed out to me how we often produce our own unhappiness by continually repeating the same destructive behavior. "The trouble with you, Lorna," she would say, "is: you hear a knock at the door, and when you open it, there stands the mailman with a package, and you grab the mailman!"

We parted at the Mother House, and I returned to the Y. After lunch, I went to my room to lie down. I couldn't stop wondering: why had God brought me to Calcutta? Why was I so attracted to the Missionaries of Charity? Was I supposed to be a nun? God, I hoped not. I decided to do something worldly immediately and went to Flury's for tea and a chocolate éclair.

Monday,
April 6, 1981

Sadly, I said good-bye to my new friends—to June, Trudi, Etienne, Blondine, Pauline and all the others who were still there. Then I went to Prem Dan to say good-bye to Meeta. When Sister Veronica explained to her I was leaving for America, she struggled up off her cot, bent over and touched my feet. I cried.

I had stopped looking at people as an amorphous collective. It was easy to discard the burned woman as one of the many hopeless statistics on a tally sheet, but my experience with her had brought into reality Mother's words, "All life, no matter how lowly or wretched, carries within it the light of the Divine and is, therefore, sacred." Some have said what Mother Teresa does is "only a drop in the ocean," to which she replies, "Yes, it's true, but the ocean would miss that particular drop if it wasn't there."

Mother asked if I would take a few packages with me to New York for the Missionaries of Charity sisters in the South Bronx.

"I'd be delighted to."

"I'll have them ready for you when you come for Adoration."

When I arrived at the Mother House for Adoration, instead of the few neat packages and bundle of letters I had envisioned, I was greeted by a gleeful Mother Teresa hopping, like Rumpelstilskin, around four enormous boxes that were almost as tall as she. It took me a few seconds to cotton to the fact that these were the "few packages." I burst out laughing at her audacity. I told her that she had some nerve expecting me to lug these boxes to London and then on to New York.

How could I possibly take these plus my own luggage? Stupid question. I know, I know, how could my luggage have any importance compared to Missionaries of Charity boxes? She laughed and said they were important boxes because they contained the Missionaries of Charity Constitution to be distributed to all the houses in the Americas. Actually, I was charmed she had entrusted me with this mission. She sat me down on the bench, patted my knee and said, "All for Jesus, all for Jesus." She was so delightfully manipulative.

Although I wasn't quite so anxious to leave Calcutta as I had been, I looked forward to the neat sanctuary of my apartment, the supposed glamour of Sotheby's, telephones, beautiful objects, high heels, manicured nails, good food and staying clean all day. I confessed all this to Mother.

"Mother, it's been an experience I wouldn't have missed for the world, but it's not one I am anxious to repeat." In my arrogance I assured her I would always be happy to see her whenever she came to New York, but I would not be returning to Calcutta again. She smiled wisely, and said she quite understood, that life in Calcutta was hard, but I should "Keep the Missionaries of Charity in my prayers and try to keep the joy of loving Jesus in my heart to share with all I meet."

She took my hand in hers and said that the Devil would constantly work on me to divert me from the spiritual path. She cautioned me not to dwell on the past but to live in the moment, "I will pray to Mary and ask her to be a Mother to you to keep you pure and holy."

The time to part had come. I kept smoothing the skirt of her sari. I wanted to hug her so badly. In truth I wanted to fling myself into her lap. No matter how many brave words I uttered, I felt like a helpless child in her presence. I knew I was going to miss her terribly, but out of respect for her, I held myself in check and saluted her with the *namaskar*. My eyes were brimming. Mother Teresa took my hands again and held them tightly and told me she wanted me to write to her and to see her when she visited New York. We said goodbye, and I left.

Paulette and several of the sisters helped me to load the boxes into the waiting van at the end of the alley on Lower Circular Road. Paulette and I hugged; I jumped into the van, and the driver pulled away.

*Sisters doing laundry in the courtyard
of the Mother House, Calcutta*

The Gumley House Chapel

A picture of my sister Pamela in the oval frame

Family portrait: My parents, my brother and I

The Mother House Chapel

In the rostrum at Sotheby's, 1980

Slums beside Prem Dan

Sister Paulette

Baloo and Nola – Prem Dan, 1983

The balcony outside the chapel at the Mother House, Calcutta

Ellen Fiorillo

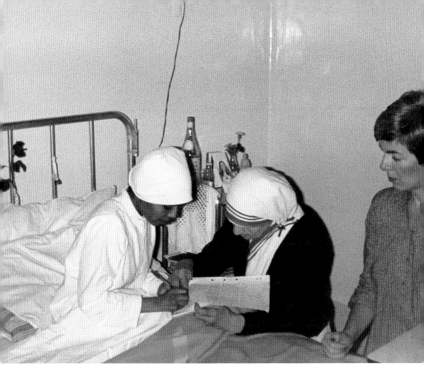

*Sister Lorna wearing her habit and kerchief, signing her
Final Vows with Mother and I kneeling by the bedside*

Mother and I in Rome, 1983

During my "Dark Night" Experience, 1993

Mother with First Group, Chapter 1997

Mother and I, Calcutta, Chapter 1997

Returning to America

Landing at London's Heathrow airport, I longed to get to my mother's house to have a decent meal and sleep, but first I had to take care of the wretched boxes and put them in the Left Luggage. What a rigmarole it turned out to be. I tried to hold on to Mother Teresa's words, "All for Jesus, all for Jesus."

My mother lived only a few miles from the airport; our difficulties three weeks before were forgotten, and I was happy to see her again. I tried to explain the Calcutta experience but wasn't exactly sure what had happened to me; it was difficult to put into words. The next day I headed back to New York. New York City appeared orderly and subdued after Calcutta. Even the rudeness of the New York cab driver was poetry to my ears, and my tiny studio apartment a haven of cleanliness and peace.

The next day, like the wedding guest at the end of Coleridge's poem "The Rime of the Ancient Mariner," I passed through Sotheby's double glass doors a "sadder and a wiser" woman than the woman who had left just three weeks before. Did I still belong in this heady, arty, affluent setting that had once meant so much to me? Here no one ate rice out of a tin bowl with her fingers or was starving or suffering with leprosy. There were no old crones to hold in my arms as they took their last breath. There were no feverish brows to stroke. There were no dark pleading eyes to look into. What was I doing here?

I tried to make light of my conflict. "Lucille, don't give me any more books about nuns; you have no idea what you started. And if I end up in the convent, I'll blame you for sabotaging a perfectly good career." Easy-going, gentle Lucille had been anxious about my going to India (fearing I'd get sick) and was overjoyed to see me. The feeling was mutual. I was happy to be back at the office in my own setting, looking through my mail, having lunch with clients. How good it felt to be back in the rostrum—as good as the first time.

But imperceptibly Calcutta had wound its way into my head and heart. I thought of it more and more. I began to be obsessed by it. It was not the novel experience I had thought I could use for conversation at smart dinner parties. It was too disturbing. However much I tried to keep the visions of Calcutta out of my daily round, they crept back. At the oddest times I found myself longing for the life I'd had there and for the refreshing order of the sisters' days. Involved at some task, at my desk, on the telephone, at lunch with clients or even in mid-auction, I'd be assailed by a memory, a feeling, a face, feeding my craving to return.

I found myself stopping by empty churches for quiet time, to sit still and reflect. I was unable to maintain the same spiritual routine I had begun with the sisters in Calcutta, and, much to my surprise, I missed it, especially early morning prayers and Adoration.

I had many dreams about Calcutta and Mother. One was particularly vivid. I was in a dimly lit basement at a cocktail party. Mother appeared, took me by the hand and led me to the exit. We ascended wide stone steps up toward the light. As we went, Mother, still holding my hand and leading the way, transformed into a young woman. She was barefoot, with long dark hair flowing down her back. She wore a Martha

Graham-like dress with long sleeves and a full skirt. She skipped lightly but determinedly up the steps. Breathlessly I tried to protest, "But Mother, I don't understand the Sacred Heart of Jesus. There are many things I don't believe."

"Oh, that doesn't matter, come on," she said as she pulled me up and out of the dark.

The desire for a spiritual life also gave me a desire for a simpler one. Working at Sotheby's had given me a first row seat in the theatre of the material and worldly. I was aware of the damage the desire for possessions could inflict on the soul, and, in reaction, I longed to keep my personal surroundings very plain. I had already had times where I delighted in throwing stuff away, getting down to the bare essentials. My experience in Calcutta served to reinforce a process I had already begun.

I became keenly aware of my excesses and extravagances. I learned to economize. Although I looked with affection at my fifty pairs of shoes, I admitted it was quite indulgent to have so many. I budgeted my time so as not to take so many taxis. Public transportation, I thought, was not only efficient but also kinder to the city. Even though I had only myself to support, I learned the joy of doing without, of not having every little thing my heart desired. I got rid of everything I didn't need.

I had kept a diary since the age of thirteen and had stored every one of them. They were an obsession, a burden. I read them through once and then burned the lot. It was a great relief. I had hoarded letters and sentimental knickknacks since my days with Aunt Lorna in Canada. I'd hauled them back and forth across the Atlantic several times; some were in boxes I hadn't opened in years. I threw them all away. I kept in my mind's eye the Missionaries of Charity who owned nothing personal; it spurred me on.

And books, those sacred cows. I had lots of good, glossy, art books which I rarely looked at but felt important to have. I realized I did not need to duplicate The New York Public Library. So every time I left the apartment, I took a pile of my books and put them on the street. By the time I returned home, every last volume had always gone. I had a satisfying sense of sending them out into the universe without controlling their destiny. I began to feel lighter.

I even toyed with the idea of having a vocation. Had I been called? Was the longing I felt sentimentality, or was it a calling from God to join the Missionaries of Charity? I couldn't tell, but I was confident God would let me know. Ever since Gumley I had been fascinated with convent life, but having a fascination is very different from a calling. Anyway, the idea of joining as a postulant was quite unappealing. Knowing my nature, I'd strive to be Mother General immediately, not exactly the right attitude for a Religious. And what about Sotheby's? Was I willing to let go of my career?

Without success I sat in my office trying to push Calcutta out of my mind. Nothing at work had the urgency or the relevance it once had. How could deciphering if an object were mid-or-late 19th century compare to the experience of the woman covered in burns or the rickshaw drivers riddled with TB, or the nuns reciting the Rosary at the Mother House? Nothing at work seemed very "weighty." I wrote to Mother:

> Dear Mother,
>
> You will be thrilled to know carting those cartons of the Constitution was not easy. However, at great risk to life and limb, I took a taxi to the South Bronx yesterday and delivered the boxes and letters to Sister Priscilla.

I was so anxious to leave Calcutta, yet now there's something missing in my life. They say once one accepts one is alcoholic, the knowledge ruins one's drinking. I have another sort of knowledge—a different life is available and possible. My old ideas have been shaken, and I know nothing will ever be the same.

A few weeks later came Mother's reply:

My dear Lorna,

Thank you for your beautiful letter. God loves you for the love you gave and the joy you shared with our sisters and the poor while in Calcutta. We all become better through the close touch with Jesus in the distressing disguise of the poor. We assure you of our prayers that you may grow in the likeness of Christ through love and compassion. Come back to Calcutta and be only all for Jesus. . . .

Come back to Calcutta? I couldn't do that. Or could I? I spent long hours in coffee shops with Ellen going over the experience again and again. "What should I do? Did I have a calling? Could I give up *everything?*" Ellen didn't think so. She felt my becoming a Religious would probably deflate my spirit, especially joining such a traditional order like the Missionaries of Charity. She didn't think that I would last long with the vow of obedience; she believed I would soon feel trapped.

"Besides," she said, "you could be far more effective being God's ambassador to the world outside a convent."

Three months after I returned from Calcutta, Mother was in the United States staying at her convent in the South Bronx; I went there with a posy of tiny roses for her. She was out, expected back any moment, but I was nervous, so I gave the flowers to Sister Priscilla and left.

The next day I came again; I was afraid Mother wouldn't want to be bothered or, worse still, she wouldn't remember me. My fears and projections were unfounded. As soon as she saw me, her eyes lit up, and she wanted to know why I hadn't waited when I delivered my roses (I noticed they were in the place of honor at the foot of the statue of the Blessed Virgin). I sobbed.

I held out for eleven months, but by February I knew I had to return. It was madness. I had no illusions about Calcutta, but the longing to go back was persistent. I took another three-week vacation and, on March 15, 1982, exactly a year to the day I first arrived there, I was again walking down the short alleyway off Lower Circular Road and pulling the bell chain of the Mother House.

Calcutta Again

Mother was in. When she saw me she looked startled for a second, then her dear, wrinkled face broke into a smile. She chuckled and said, "I knew you'd be back." I burst into tears.

Here I was sobbing again, and again *she* was chuckling. I stood before her loving everything about her: her rounded shoulders, her head bent as if she carried a great weight, the wimple low over her brow, her wonderful hands, the crucifix on her shoulder, her habit always shorter than those of the other nuns—ballerina length.

Once again I stayed at the Y, this time in a room overlooking the tennis courts. The furniture was the same, the bed as bumpy and as active as before. The same waiters: surly Raja with a sergeant major's moustache, Sukomal, the toast burner, and Nissar the chef. The cuisine hadn't improved one iota, but none of it bothered me.

Seeing Paulette, I felt as though a week had passed rather than a year. We spent afternoons just as we had the year before, talking about everything under the sun. Sister Ursha was still at Prem Dan. She had been very ill and was obliged to relinquish her responsibilities as Superior. She told me Meeta, the burned woman, had healed and left Prem Dan a month after I returned to America. She didn't know where she'd gone. Sister Veronica had been transferred to Bangladesh.

I revisited Kalighat and delved right into work. Sister Luke was still in charge; the beds were still full, different people, same problems. It brought to mind Jesus saying to Judas: "For you have the poor always with you." (Matt. 26:11). I was aware I didn't feel quite as detached as I had before, nor did irritation well up in me so easily. I was mindful they were my brothers and sisters; the patients, at once wretched and dear, had exacted compassion from my slowly opening heart.

The situation in Calcutta was still as dismal but did not appear to me as hopeless. It was not Calcutta that had changed. I saw the Missionaries of Charity with new eyes too. The year before I had perceived them as rare birds, quite in tune with the Almighty. Now I saw them more realistically, as women developing and maturing along the spiritual path as I was. I saw they too, like me, were in a process and had by no means arrived.

One evening Mother was to take a flight to Delhi. I drove with her out to the airport only to find her flight had been delayed an hour. If I had been in that same situation, I probably would have sat down and read a magazine for an hour, but Mother, never wasting a minute, decided to visit one of the Missionaries of Charity centers nearby.

The sisters were at supper when we arrived, and because I, as an outsider, could not go into the refectory, Mother, ever thoughtful, put her head around the curtain and asked the sisters to come outside. When they saw her, they burst into high-pitched squeals and yelps of "Mother, Mother!"

Like puppies out of a basket they came tumbling over one another, giggling and squealing, their heads bowed in anticipation of Mother's blessing. Mother did nothing to stop them, and I wondered why. Probably, I thought, because she's far more accepting and tolerant than I am and doesn't interfere with any process, however trivial or exasperating. She allows the Holy Spirit to mold and form souls to His Will.

The squealing eventually died down. It was dusk; we sat under a large tree and Mother, with her odd mixture of the spiritual and the practical, asked the sisters if they were staying close to the Blessed Virgin and what vegetables they were growing. They told her about the vegetables and about how good the Blessed Virgin was to them and how happy they were. Sitting at Mother's feet, they were having a grand old time.

As the minutes ticked by, fearing Mother would miss her plane, I became anxious to leave. I reminded her we should get going. She agreed and stood. Then, of course, she had to bless every last one of them again! I could feel my desire to control her and my irritation increase with every blessing. I tried to steer her towards the car, but her devoted flock kept distracting her. After what seemed an eon, Mother reached the car, and just as she was about to get in, the sister-in-charge mentioned that a baby in the nursery was dying. Mother stopped in her tracks and asked that the child be brought to her.

I was over the top. I tutted and sighed with the unspoken attitude of "We don't have time for dying babies; you have a plane to catch!" Mother, gently placed her hand on my arm, and quietly said, "I will come soon, but I must see the child."

I was completely disarmed. She didn't point out how rude and inconsiderate and impatient I was. She was able to see through my rudeness, to see Jesus in his distressing disguise as the badly mannered.

The tiny, dying baby was brought to her. As she held the frail bundle in her arms, my anxiety and vexation dissolved. She said a prayer and tucked a Miraculous Medal into the infant's clothing before handing her back to the sister. It didn't matter to Mother if she ever made the flight. What was important to her was attending to the child God had placed in front of her at that moment. Only that was important.

When Mother returned from her trip, we once again sat on the little bench outside the office. She told me about new Missionaries of Charity houses opening all over the world. A house in Russia was her greatest wish. She had little time these days to spend doing hands-on work with her precious poor. Her effort each day was taken up with being a mother to the over three thousand sisters in the Order, with overseeing administration, with signing documents and with prayer, prayer, prayer.

I told her how my experience in Calcutta had influenced me. My job no longer had the appeal it once had, and I found it all rather disturbing. She told me that once we set foot on His path, we must be willing to let God use us in any way according to His will. She warned me to be prepared: "You will be asked to relinquish things you consider most dear and, when those times come, accept whatever God gives or takes with an open and free heart."

I told her I had not wanted to return to Calcutta but some force had drawn me, and I had no idea why. She responded, "Spiritual maturity is not waiting for things to *feel* right. We do things because we know they *are* right."

Three weeks had passed and it was time to leave again. Paulette and Sister Joseph got permission to see me off at the airport. It wasn't as it had been before; this time I knew I'd be back.

Closing Doors

I didn't really have much say in my destiny. Change has its own momentum. When I returned to New York from Calcutta this second time, my worst fears were realized: my love affair with Sotheby's was over. I still loved the auctions, but I could no longer work up any enthusiasm for budgets, catalog layouts or collections. No longer was I interested in what works of art were for sale, and I rarely visited the exhibitions. I knew I had to let go of Sotheby's. I couldn't hold on to one thing hoping for something else to come into my life—clutching rhinestones to my breast while God awaits with diamonds—I had to let it all go. I agonized over the decision. Sotheby's was my home, my life, my family, my harbor. It was where I'd gone every working day for the past thirteen years. I balked at the prospect of not having it in my life any more. I needed help. One day help arrived. I went to see John Marion, President of Sotheby's, and to my utter surprise, he fired me.

I walked out of the building stunned at the speed of this change. I recalled Mother's words about "God taking things away." I would never have been able to leave of my own accord, and I could see the wisdom in using John to move me on, but still I felt breathless at the speed of it all. I was also hurt and bewildered.

I had seen John Marion in the rostrum my first day at Sotheby's. I was mesmerized as I watched him encourage and cajole bidders, all the while keeping up a boisterous pace. It was all so theatrical. It was John Marion who gave me my break and allowed me to be an auctioneer. Did he like me or not? Was he friend or foe? I didn't understand. There was the incident at the Plaza. He'd stood by me then when he could easily, even justifiably, have fired me.

I had been sober for only three months and was a fledging auctioneer when a philanthropic organization that had planned an auction and gala dinner at the Plaza Hotel asked Sotheby's to provide a professional. I agreed to do the job before checking what was for sale, how many lots were to be offered and how the event was to be organized—a mistake I would never repeat.

Fund-raisers often assume an auction is a simple process. The uninitiated are unaware of the meticulous organization that goes into mounting an auction—that unless the proceedings are carried out with the precision of a space launch, the event can turn into a fiasco. Filled with enthusiasm and self-importance at the prospect of performing at the Plaza Hotel, I went barreling along a perilous course.

The evening arrived. I had bought a new dress, had my hair styled and my make-up professionally applied. I felt like a million dollars as I waltzed into the Plaza, up the gilded staircase and into a room where a throng was gathering. And what a throng! Fabulous jewels flashed and sparkled from wrists, necks, ears, bosoms. Designer gowns were everywhere. My million-dollar feeling began ebbing away. These were rich New Yorkers engaged in the light, frothy chatter of the socially elevated. I was not one of them. I had an old feeling of being excluded but quickly reminded myself I had a job to do; I couldn't waste time comparing my lot with theirs. Besides, pretty soon all eyes would be on me alone.

The glitterati flowed into the dining room and were seated. Before dinner was served, a frantic lady in a frantic dress made the announcement that the auction would begin right now. Oh no! A hungry audience held hostage—the worst. I was led to a small platform and was told by the Frantic One, who was obviously in charge, to begin.   Suddenly, without any preparation, I was on. There was no catalog, no sequence to follow, none of the props and tools employed for the smooth running of the Sotheby's sales room.

The first item was one of Bella Abzug's hats.   No fine piece of silver or Picasso print, but a shapeless, second-hand felt hat. Bravely, I commenced.   By this time it was obvious to me the hungry and impatient audience did not want to be subjected to an auction.   They were there to meet their friends and were about as interested in Ms. Abzug's chapeau as I was. They would not keep quiet. The hubbub increased as people tried to find their seats or greet each other with lots of exclaiming, kissing of cheeks and embracing.   Waiters taking and delivering drink orders added to the confusion.   People in the rear of the room were shouting at those in front to keep quiet and to sit down. The scene verged on chaos. The Frantic One developed acute hysteria.

Three times I asked for quiet, but no one heard me.   I was accustomed to having everyone's rapt attention, and here I was facing bedlam. I gazed at the rowdy throng helplessly. Would they ever stop talking? Over fifty lots to sell, and I couldn't get through the first one. Once again, I entreated them for silence—to no avail.   Then I knew I couldn't continue unless I had a vodka and orange juice. I would have to drink.   A moment of desperate reckoning and. . . it wasn't worth it. Whatever the cost, I would not drink. I would not go backwards. I turned the microphone level up to its limit and said, "Ladies and Gentlemen, I can no longer afford to be here."

I gathered up my shawl and walked through the crowd right out of the room. The sudden silence was deafening. I left all four hundred revelers sitting there in the Plaza Hotel.

No one followed me out.   Soon I was in the cool evening air racing towards home. I tore off the new dress and, like a frightened child, scrubbed my face, donned a fleecy, comforting nightgown and jumped into bed, pulling the covers over my head. I told myself over and over that everything was all right. I was sober. I hadn't had a drink. I remembered Ellen's words, "No matter what happens, or how you feel, if you put your head on the pillow at night and haven't had a drink that day, you're a success."

But still I couldn't shake the thunderous boom of my heart beat and in my head the terrible anticipation of the consequences of my action. I imagined John Marion assembling the staff in the main sales room to witness my fall. To the continuous rat-a-tat-tat of a drum, he would slap me across the face with a catalog, break my gavel across his knee and order me onto a waiting tumbrel that would transport me down Madison Avenue, past all the solemn-faced dealers and clients to THE UNEMPLOYMENT OFFICE.

The fall-out didn't occur for a few days. I had intended to relate the entire saga to John at the first opportunity but thought he was out of town for the week. When I finally did call him, he'd already heard about it from the Frantic One. He told me to be in his office at nine-thirty sharp the following morning. I was terrified.

I met Ellen for coffee and could hardly sit still. She told me the world had not come to an end. Those four hundred people had continued with their lives and were not still sitting at the Plaza waiting for me. She said I'd made the right choice and encouraged me to trust in the Divine Right Order of things.

The next morning, dressed in a black velvet suit and white blouse (appropriate attire for a beheading), I arrived in John's office at the appointed hour. He sat behind his desk and listened to my account of the fiasco. When I had finished, he took a deep breath and lightly admonished me for taking on a job without fully investigating it beforehand. I was taken by surprise; more, I had the distinct impression that beneath the obligatory reprimand were respect and admiration. He admired my audacity; he didn't say so, but his manner was one of barely disguised amusement. Oh, joyous relief! John Marion was on my side.

Now, six years later, he'd fired me. Why? He said the company was cutting back. I didn't believe it. I knew Sotheby's was "cutting back," but I didn't believe *that* was the reason. I was a top auctioneer. I made a lot of money for the company. So why? What was the real reason? This question would niggle me for a long time.

A few weeks later, I packed my personal belongings into boxes, took the elevator from the fourth floor to the lobby, walked across the speckled marble floor through the double glass doors and out onto Madison Avenue. No one in the company was told I was fired. No memo was sent. Nothing formal was announced. After thirteen years, with trials and triumphs, I just sort of faded away. It was an ignominious end to a wonderful career. I had no idea where I was going or what lay ahead of me, and, in the grand scheme of things, it mattered not a jot.

Waiting

I believed, with no small measure of spiritual arrogance, that as soon as I broke with Sotheby's, some miraculous opportunity would be presented to me. Within a couple of weeks at the most, I would be receiving something like a gold-rimmed card in the mail inscribed, "Dearest Lorna, I have a special mission just for you. Meet me in Jerusalem. Love, God." I was so sure I would be employed in the services of the Lord very shortly, and I wouldn't have a thing to worry about. Of course, it would be a glorious mission: something to equal leading the Israelites out of Egypt or Gandhi's freedom movement in India—something to set the world on its ear.

Nothing of the sort happened. No card arrived, no burning bushes, no parting of the East River. Nothing. Instead, I went from a life of appointments, gallery openings, clients, and lunches, to one of solitude and meditation. At first it was fine. It was an opportunity to be quiet, to practice doing just what the day presented, a time for reflection and listening. I was learning the great art of doing nothing. I learned how to be still—my greatest challenge.

In my second year of "the great art of doing nothing," I made several attempts to be gainfully employed, but each door I approached was shut. Doing nothing had ceased to be a choice; I was now being *forced* to do nothing. I flung myself even more faithfully into the Everlasting Arms and allowed myself to be carried. Since I didn't seem to be able to work,

I informed God that if these doors remained shut, He would have to support me. I had no idea how that would happen, but I had complete faith it would. I also had my own experience to lean on. I had never been without food, shelter, or clothes. I was in His care and was sure all the details of my life would be attended to. They were.

I had enough money; I even continued to keep a little savings. Of course, not working, my expenses were reduced considerably. I no longer needed to spend money on manicures and pedicures, expensive haircuts, pantyhose, high-heels or shoe repairs. Money just seemed to come to me as I needed it. I received a tax refund out of the blue. A painting I'd purchased at auction resold for over three thousand dollars when I had expected it to fetch much less. A year after I left Sotheby's, I received a call from the accounting department informing me I had not collected my last paycheck.

After the third year, however, doubts and fears that had been in hiding came to the fore. Why wasn't I being used? Although I did some volunteer work in the AIDS unit of a local hospital, I still felt as though I were operating on two cylinders and that one endless day was dragging into another. Why hadn't God called me? Maybe I wasn't quite the material He wanted. Maybe I wasn't worthy. Maybe I had been too arrogant in thinking He would. Why would God want me in any case? What did I have that was so special? Who did I think I was? I should have fought to stay at Sotheby's. I should have paid more attention to my career. All this was happening to me because I'd seen a few hungry people in India and some nuns with darns on their headwear. I wrote to Mother of my despair, and she replied, "Keep clinging to our Lord, for you know he loves you with a tender love."

I tried to cling to Him, but I felt He'd moved away. I couldn't reach Him. I sat with the feelings. I had a recurring dream. I had been selected for God's special service and was being trained for an important mission. One day an official came to review the troops, to select those few destined for God's priority work, and as the official walked along the line-up, he passed me over. He just walked by. I didn't quite measure up for Special Duty; somehow I didn't quite make the grade. I persevered with the meditation and prayer.

Another letter from Mother:

> Your feeling of being "passed over" by God—this is the sign of greater love. Do not be afraid. You are precious to Him. He loves you, only be faithful in your life of prayer and sacrifice. Don't be afraid, Jesus has drawn you in tenderness and love to Himself. I am praying for you.

It was May of 1983, and thirteen months had passed since my last visit to Calcutta. Mother Teresa was due to be in Rome. I wanted to see her again.

It was a glorious spring and my first time in Rome; the city was exuberant, warm, ancient. Mother was staying in one of her houses in a poor suburb. I boarded the Metro, then a bus and, with much mouthing, gesticulating and showing a small picture of Mother to the locals, I was directed to the convent and rang the bell on the courtyard gate. An Indian sister I didn't know opened a small door, and I passed through.

To my immediate right were a tiny garden area with little benches under a few shade trees and a small patch of grass surrounded with flowerbeds. Next to the garden a chapel with the doors wide open to the courtyard. I could see Mother's back as she knelt in prayer. She was alone. I went and knelt beside her. She looked up; her eyes widened in surprise, and her face broke into a welcoming smile. Without speaking she patted my arm and returned to her prayers for a few minutes.

Once outside she greeted me warmly. I couldn't speak. I looked at her closely, and although her face was old and lined, her expression was youthful. Sometimes when she smiled, I'd see an inquiring look cross her face, and I felt I was seeing Agnes. Maybe I was seeing the same expression her parents and brother and sisters saw when she was a young girl. Presently she was on retreat, spending time with the sisters who were to take Final Vows in a few days, but right now, she said, she was preparing to go out to a hospital to visit a sister who was ill. Would I come along?

A round Italian priest turned up in a small Fiat. Mother, two sisters and I squeezed in, and off we drove. No sooner had we pulled away than Mother made the Sign of the Cross and we recited a few prayers—never an idle moment.

At the hospital the doctor and head nurse, a nun from the order that ran the hospital, greeted us. They escorted us through the clean, spacious corridors amidst much excitement. Word was out Mother Teresa was here. We entered a ward with six patients. The ailing sister was behind a white bed-screen. Mother chuckled and introduced us, "Lorna, I'd like you to meet *Sister* Lorna."

Sister Lorna was Indian, young and exceptionally beautiful with large, luminous eyes and a delicate, heart-shaped face. She had perfect teeth and never stopped smiling. She looked angelic, all in white, lying against white pillows covered with white sheets, physically weak yet exploding with joy. On her night table were a crucifix and several religious pictures as well as a statue of the Blessed Virgin that glowed in the dark. Rosary beads were wound about her fingers. I could not tell what exactly was wrong with her, something to do with her heart perhaps. To all Mother's inquiries about her health, she insisted she was fine and happy to be spending so much time with Jesus.

I learned she was one of the sisters scheduled to take Final Vows, and Mother had been anxious to see her, not so much because she was ill but because she was without vows—her vows had expired. During their formation, a nun takes vows for periods of a year or two; only Final Vows are permanent. Sister Lorna would not be well enough to attend the Professions ceremony, so Mother wanted her to take her vows then and there. Mother asked if she might have a piece of paper and was handed a lined pad. She began to write the vow but then pushed the pad towards me.

"You write it, please. You have nice handwriting."

Mother and I knelt by the bed. She dictated. I wrote.

> In the name of the Father and of the Son and of the Holy Spirit. Amen.
>
> For the Honor and Glory of God, and moved by a burning desire to quench the infinite thirst of Jesus on the Cross for love of souls, by consecrating myself more fully to God, that I may follow Jesus more closely in my whole life in a spirit of loving trust, total surrender and cheerfulness, here and now, in the presence of Lorna Kelly, and into your hands, Mother Teresa, Superior General of the Society of the Missionaries of Charity, I, Sister Lorna, vow for life, Chastity, Poverty, Obedience and Wholehearted and Free Service to the poorest of the poor according to the Constitutions of the Missionaries of Charity.
>
> I give myself with my whole heart to this religious family, so that by the grace of the Holy Spirit and the help of the Immaculate Heart of Mary, Cause of Our Joy and Queen of the World, I may be led to the perfect love of God and neighbor and make the Church fully present in the world of today.

Sister Lorna read the vow out loud, signed it; then Mother signed it and blessed her. That done, Mother's mind was on to the next thing. We got to our feet and left Sister Lorna to savor her life with her new spouse. With only Mother and a stranger as her witness, Sister Lorna had committed herself for the rest of her life.

The doctor asked Mother if she would visit some other patients.

"Of course," was her quick reply, and we set off on a short tour of the hospital. Mother gave time and blessings to each patient, moving on quickly and yet giving her undivided attention. She was a great politician. The sisters who ran the hospital invited her to their convent nearby. Mother accepted and asked if I too could go inside. The Superior welcomed me in with a wave of her arm.

We were shown to the chapel and Mother, without hesitation, sank to her knees to pray for a few minutes. We were then escorted to see a sister who, a hundred-and-one years old, had been a nun for over eighty years. She was sitting in a chair, a little net bonnet on her head and a shawl around her shoulders. She knew exactly who Mother Teresa was and was so happy to meet her. It was charming to see Mother, an old lady herself, bending over to greet another, much older lady, who had already been a nun for over ten years when Mother was born.

Eventually we were ushered into a room where a magnificent tea was laid out on a beautifully set table: white linen napkins and a lace tablecloth, little sandwiches, cream cakes and a pot of good-smelling tea. Oh good, I was feeling quite peckish. But alas, it was not to be. Mother Teresa had other thoughts—higher thoughts than mine, for to my dismay I heard her say, "Oh no, I'm sorry."

"Please, Mother, have a sandwich, a piece of cake, we've set it out for you," implored the Superior.

"I can't. Thank you so much, you're very kind but, because of my vow to identify with the poor, I don't take food outside."

"Oh, of course, of course," sighed the well-padded Superior. As we left the room, I cast a longing, backward glance at the cream cakes.

I had planned to stay in Rome only a few days, but I was entranced by the city, and Mother was there, so I stayed for two weeks. The day of Professions arrived. The ceremony took place in a large modern church on the outskirts of Rome. It was packed with relatives and friends and the sisters from the various Missionaries of Charity houses in Rome. A bishop officiated with at least ten priests in attendance. There was much singing and praying as about twenty-five young women filed in with Mother behind them.

From a semi-circle formed around the altar, each nun in turn stepped forward and recited the same vow I had written for Sister Lorna, and then signed her document on the altar. Mass and more singing followed. When it was over, the priests and the newly consecrated "Brides of Christ" proceeded from the church with Mother in the rear holding the signed documents.

The ceremony was followed by a reception in the gardens of the Missionaries of Charity convent at Casilina. It was a perfect Roman day, comfortably hot with intense blue skies. The sisters welcomed the new brides by placing a garland of bright flowers around their necks and performing an Indian ceremonial dance in their honor. They sang and glided in a graceful column, carrying aloft dishes of lighted candles surrounded with blossoms.

Mother was leaving Rome the next day for a week, so while she was away I decided to visit Florence—a pretty city crammed with art, but I didn't have the heart for it. Flitting around Florence felt like a waste of time. I was bored, agitated and happy to get back to Rome.

When Mother returned from her trip, she stayed at her convent in San Gregorio, close by the Coliseum, where the Missionaries of Charity took care of homeless women. I called, and Mother answered the telephone, "Are you busy?" she asked. "Can you come and see me right now?"

I hailed a taxi and dashed over.

When I arrived, Mother explained that one of the sisters was being transferred to Gaza and was leaving the next day. She knew I planned to go to Israel after Rome, but as I had no set itinerary, asked if I would accompany the sister to Gaza via Cairo. Absolutely, I said. As well as the usual packet of letters for the sisters, Mother gave me a card with an ink drawing of two fishermen casting a net over the side of their boat, on it she wrote, "You and Jesus, together in one boat catching souls. God bless you. M. Teresa, M.C." I went off to the airline office to make arrangements.

At the airport the next day, two of the sisters met me and introduced me to Sister Daniel, a young American sister from Buffalo, New York. She and I boarded the plane for Cairo, and as soon as we'd taken our seats, she took out her rosary and said a decade. A meal was served. It was the first time I'd dined with a Missionaries of Charity sister. Fork in hand, Sister Daniel dove at the plate as if she had to spear the food in case it escaped. She bent over the tray and, in a flash, gobbled up every morsel. When she lifted her head there wasn't a cracker, a piece of parsley or a trace of gravy left. I was a fast eater, but petite Sister Daniel outstripped me easily. I couldn't resist a comment, whereupon she informed me the sisters were taught not to leave a thing on their plates out of love for the poor. I wondered if that were indeed the case, or if she had simply been hungry.

A priest met us at the airport in Cairo and drove us to the Missionaries of Charity convent in a very poor section of the city. The convent was just a few rooms on the second floor of a dilapidated apartment building. Even though space was limited, one of the rooms had been converted into a chapel with the familiar **I Thirst** next to the crucifix on the wall. We left Sister Daniel there, and I was shown to lodgings nearby.

The following morning I took a bus with Sister Joan (the Superior), Sister Daniel, and two other sisters to the edge of the city where, stretching for acres, was an enormous garbage heap. The mission of the sisters in Cairo was working with the people who lived here. It was a grim, horrifying place. The people who picked through the garbage lived right on it. Some had carved caves out of the matted refuse; others had built shaky shelters from bits of cardboard and tin.

The smell was indescribable—absolutely foul. It was difficult to say how thick the pile was, maybe twenty or thirty feet of rotting waste. I watched with revulsion as Sister Joan in her sandaled feet strode out across the refuse. I, too, was wearing sandals; I took a deep breath and followed her. My feet sank into the spongy, hot mess. I fixed my attention elsewhere. Children, barefoot, were buzzing everywhere like marauding flies. Only the youngest were playing; the older ones were busily sorting through heaps of stuff, separating cans from glass, plastic from paper.

Grubby black pigs rooted about happily. Scruffy, half-starved donkeys pulled in cartload after cartload of still more refuse while other children supervised the operation. Sister Joan told me that thousands of families lived here and that over two thousand tons of refuse were collected and dumped here daily. She said the community had been on this dump for over a hundred years; they ate from it, dressed from it, and lived in it. It was a sort of hell.

We trekked about ten minutes and came to the dispensary, a rather substantial building compared to the other shacks. It was here the sisters took care of the dump dwellers' ailments. Today they were dealing with the children—a hardy bunch. That any baby survived at all seemed miraculous. There were the usual boils, sores, rashes and bellies full of worms. Sister Joan left the sisters to carry on with the work and took me to meet Sister Emmanuelle.

I knew of Sister Emmanuelle. She was seventy-four years old and belonged to a French teaching order. She had been a college professor until the age of sixty-two when, because of her health, she was advised to retire. Not ready to lead a sedentary life and not at all worried about her health, she had asked God to send her to serve Him in the most wretched place on earth. Like Father Damien with the lepers and Mother Teresa with the poorest of the poor,

Sister Emmanuelle had committed her life to serving the outcasts on the Cairo garbage dump.

After our introductions, Sister Emmanuelle told Sister Joan about a problem in the community. Both spoke in a mixture of French and Arabic, making it impossible for me to understand anything they said. After minutes of animated chatter, Sister Emmanuelle asked us to follow her, and along the way Sister Joan explained the conversation. A Christian girl had been seen alone with a Muslim boy. Most of the people on the dump were Coptic Christians, and if a girl were seen with a Muslim boy, it brought dishonor and disgrace to her family. A Muslim boy would never want to marry her, and her own community would shun her. Now her brother wanted to kill her to avenge the family name. Here they were, living in the garbage, and people were worried about their family name! Incredibly, even the girl's grandfather was considering cutting her throat.

We arrived at a rough wooden shed where an Orthodox priest was outside talking to the girl's grandfather. The old man was very agitated; he pulled a key from the folds of a filthy brown *djellaba* and unlocked the padlock on the shed door. When we entered the dark space, it took a few moments for my eyes to adjust to the gloom, and then I saw a young girl on a pile of garbage in a corner with her hands tied behind her back.

She was fifteen years old and had been in the shed for three days without food. Everyone was speaking at once; I couldn't understand a word. The priest untied the girl's hands and told her to stand in the middle of the space. He started shouting at her. She said nothing but held her head in a defiant pose. I could tell she was prepared to die. It was eerie.

Suddenly the priest hauled back and slapped her so hard

across her face she went sprawling on the ground. Neither Sister Joan nor Sister Emmanuelle moved or said a word. Shocked though I was, it was apparent some plan was afoot, and not interfering was the best course of action. Their single focus was to save the girl's life. She got back on her feet and with great dignity brushed off her dirty, ragged skirt as though it were a ball gown and silently stood her ground.

The priest shouted again and slapped her again, not quite so hard. He took a lump of bread from his pocket and flung it on the ground at her feet, yelling all the while. Then we left. The old man seemed satisfied. A few days later Sister Joan informed me the priest had convinced the grandfather to release the girl to his charge and that she was now safely away from the dump and in the care of a family on the other side of Cairo.

Sister Daniel and I continued our journey. We crossed the Sinai leaving Cairo by bus early in the morning to avoid the heat. I crossed the Israeli border without any problem, but Sister Daniel was taken into a room and made to strip. Apparently a bishop had been caught a few months earlier smuggling weapons under his robes, so the guards were suspicious of any one in religious garb.

When we arrived at the Missionaries of Charity in Gaza, I had a light meal and a long sleep. In the late afternoon I took a taxi to Jerusalem. I felt sorry for Sister Daniel, plonked down in the middle of a troubled zone and having to learn Arabic; it was a far cry from Buffalo.

Early in June I was back in New York. I wrote Mother about how happy I was to have seen her in Rome. I reported on the sisters in Cairo and Gaza and wrote that I still didn't know what to do with myself, but I was trying to stay open and move as the spirit moved me.

She replied to my letter:

> . . . be very careful of living by the spirit. It can be very dangerous, as the Devil, the father of lies, can come to you as an angel of light and cheat you with your eyes wide open. Keep the joy of being loved by Jesus as your strength and share it with all whose lives you are called to touch with His healing love.

Reconciliation

December '83 found me again in India. Again I stayed at the Y. Mother Teresa was at home the entire time. I had been sober for seven years, and although I did not have the same calling or the same devout love of my religion she had, we shared a passion and sense of orthodoxy. Mother frequently said she loved all religions but was *in love* with her own. I told her how for me every day was different, not always pleasant, sometimes painful, but never boring. There were also stretches of sheer joy, but of one thing I was sure: there was no arriving; every horizon I reached just revealed another one. She agreed, "It's the same in the life of a Religious; there are many ups and downs, peaks and valleys, but there's always room to grow and it's always rewarding." I remembered Sister Dominga once saying to me that if people really knew what joy there is in convent life, "they would be lined up around the corner trying to get in."

Sister Paulette was now Superior in charge of Prem Dan. She had a huge responsibility, but she still managed to go to the villages. We took a few trips together, and she invited me to spend Christmas with her at Prem Dan.

Giant vats of curry and rice had been prepared, and Christmas morning, as I approached Prem Dan, there was a line of people, mostly women, with tin containers, snaking back over the bridge. Paulette had bought saris and new *longhis* for the patients. Music blared out from loud speakers, and Baloo, looking like a badly wrapped gift in her new sari, was dancing with Angela in the courtyard.

I sensed Paulette had changed; the rebel I loved was becoming self-willed and stubborn. She was not so easy to talk to, not so open. It was obvious to me she was becoming more and more dissatisfied with her life within the Missionaries of Charity. I urged her to talk to her sisters and to Mother about her feelings but was always met with, "They wouldn't understand." I thought she was in a rut and unwilling to change. I could feel our friendship shifting.

In 1985 Lucille Defino, who had been my secretary at Sotheby's, died of stomach cancer—a horrible, painful death. It was a tremendous loss. She had loyally stood by me through my trials. Lucille had been baffled as to why I hadn't fought to stay at Sotheby's and why I had let it go so easily; she so wanted me to be a career woman.

That same year, as I turned forty, I suddenly felt a deep longing for my own mother, my flesh-and-blood mother. I had not spent much time with her since I had left home at eighteen; she had visited me several times in New York and had seen me in the rostrum, but since my father's death, I had used my mother's house only as a transit stop—a place to sleep and change my clothes. Now I needed, and wanted, to get closer to her, but I didn't quite know how to go about it. As an adult I had never given my mother my time, and I didn't know how to bridge the years. I decided to go home for three weeks with no other plans but to be with her and to see what happened.

My mother had a problem with alcohol. She mellowed as she grew older but was full of fear. She had married at twenty-one and lost her first child. I don't think she ever fully experienced her grief over Pamela. She was now a widow living alone, with none of her three children nearby. She was confused. With her advancing alcoholism I am sure she felt isolated and misunderstood.

When my mother was in her early forties, her own mother died, and she came into a modest inheritance and was generous with family and friends. Within a few years the money had gone, most of it drunk away. Eight years later, her twin, my Aunt Lorna, died very suddenly of a heart attack. Two years after that blow, her brother died. She became depressed and made a serious suicide attempt. Then my father died. Her drinking accelerated. She was now a sloppy drunk, the type that causes scenes. Friends drifted away.

One morning crossing a busy street, she was hit by a car, and the accident left her with a permanent leg injury. Her addiction took on a different character. She started taking pills—she "ate her drinks" in the form of prescribed painkillers. Now she became even more isolated, spending many of her days and nights alone in her flat, lying on her bed and popping pills. One day her refill prescription did not arrive in the mail, and the drugs ran out; she went into withdrawal and had a fatal stroke. The death certificate read: **Cause of Death: Heart Failure**—the truth, but not the whole truth.

During my visit I sat by her bed and crocheted. We talked, we argued, we laughed, we were quiet. I went over the family photo album and asked her questions about her childhood, her friends, and events in her life. I asked her to tell me about her parents and grandparents, about the house where she grew up, about how she met father. I focused my attention on her. I took an interest in her. We had a new relationship. It was the first time I allowed myself just to be with her rather than always running away. I was determined not to judge her, to accept her as she was, to focus on the positive rather than the negative, to recall with her the happy times and the special things she did for me, for example: teaching me how to knit and how to make cakes, painstakingly helping me make paper flowers I needed for a school project, allowing me to get my ears pierced. I was grateful both she and father had supported my going to America when I was only eighteen.

I was also able to let go of an old grudge and was truthful about the year I'd spent with my aunt in Canada. I confessed how awful it had been. My mother was shocked; she knew her sister was rather eccentric but loved her very much and had been heart-broken when she died. She said she and father had no idea I had been so unhappy.

It was, however, my dead sister Pamela who effected the major breakthrough for me with my mother. Pamela had died of meningitis at the age of three—when my parents were in their mid-twenties and five years before I was born. With Pamela's death my father became disillusioned with God and stopped going to church. Neither of my parents ever returned to the gravesite after the funeral. Many times I asked my mother to take me, but she put me off with any number of weak excuses. If she would not come with me, I decided, I would find my sister's grave myself.

I called my uncle, my father's brother, who had been at Pamela's funeral forty-five years before, and he gave me directions to Woodgrange Park Cemetery, East Ham, London.

I entered the cemetery through rusty iron gates set into a high brick wall that surrounded the area—it was horribly run-down. Adding to the desolation, a gutted chapel just inside the gates stood forlorn and windowless. I despaired of finding her grave.

A little way past the chapel and to the left of the gates, was an office. I knocked and opened the door; inside the messy room, their muddy feet on the desk, were a couple of brawny gravediggers eating lunch. When I told them what I wanted, they couldn't have been more obliging, pulling an enormous ledger from a shelf with **1940** stenciled on its spine. One of them dusted the volume with his sleeve and leafed through until he found **FEBRUARY**. Then, running his index finger down the page, he stopped: **Pamela Marion Murphy, born December 29, 1936, died February 29, 1940. Area 6025, plot 25.**

Leaving his half-eaten sandwich, he took up a machete and walked me past the ruined chapel. He said it had been set on fire by vandals years before. We kept walking and came upon an area where fresh graves gaped at us between manicured mounds with fresh flowers. He said parts of the cemetery had been without any burials for many years, and now the old graves were being turned over and the land reclaimed for a new cemetery. Rather grisly, I thought.

We walked down gravel paths into another area—a densely silent area. The paths were strewn with rubbish. One could hardly see the graves beneath the overgrown grass and brambles. There were benches along the way, weeds struggling through the broken slats. The trees that bordered the paths were choked with ivy; the grasses on either side were as high as our heads, and occasionally I could see the stone tips of angels' wings above a grave, or a carved cloth-draped urn or a cherub peeking through. No visitors or relatives had come to tend these graves for years.

We arrived at a corner that didn't look any different from any other corner we had passed. My companion stopped, paced out about thirty feet, made a left, and then strode, heavy-booted, into the grasses, beating the brambles and weeds aside with his machete. He uncovered a little marker painted **6023**, then walked to the right over two graves and started slashing away the brambles from around a black marble slab. Then he left me, alone.

I tore the tenacious ivy off the stone and was amazed to see names of family members—grandparents, great-uncles, great-aunts—names I had heard my mother speak of so often. I did not know there was a family plot. At the bottom of the stone, the very last name engraved was that of my sister followed by the dates of her birth and death and then the words ***God took our darling daughter to dwell with Him above.***

I stood by that gravestone shaking with emotion as I imagined my young, confused parents standing in exactly the same spot forty-five years before, burying their "darling daughter."

I grew up. I realized my parents had not come into this world solely to be my parents. Being my parents was not their mission, only a *part* of their lives: lives, like everyone else's, shaped by events and circumstances, by joys and sorrows, and this particular sorrow must have been cruelly hard for them to shoulder. I stood there a long while. I prayed for my sister, for my parents, and for myself and thought of those events that had touched and shaped my life long before I came on the scene.

When I returned to my mother's flat, I told her I had found the grave. She asked me if I had cried; I told her I had. I told her about my feelings, how I had imagined her and father's devastation. I cried all over again. Then my mother started to talk to me about Pamela. She told me how she had contracted meningitis on a train to Wales where she was taking her to get away from the bombing in London. She told me how the disease had struck quickly, and she had dashed back to London to get Pamela into a hospital only to be told it was too late. It was wartime, and my father was unable to get time off from his duties, so she had to cope on her own. Pamela was dead within four days. Stunned, they took her in a little white coffin to the cemetery and clung to each other at the graveside and wept. Now she wept again—great heaving sobs. Years and years of pain spilled out. She fell into my arms, and I held my mother for the first time since I was little. I held her and she held me. I felt her hair against my cheek and looked directly into her blue eyes, and I knew I loved her.

My mother died December 7, 1987. After her death I stood alone in her flat and looked out at the afternoon. My heart ached for her life. If the disease of alcoholism had not killed her once-lively curiosity, she might have seen from her windows the horses grazing in the fields near the wooded park, the autumn smoke drifting, lingering in the near-bare trees.

I felt her passing keenly, and I still feel sorrow every time I think of how her life might have been had she been granted the gift of surrendering the alcohol and pills. When my mother was rushed to the hospital the day she died, she had pleaded with the nurse on duty, "Please give me a pill. I am addicted to them and must have one."

I am able to take some measure of comfort in knowing that before she died, my mother took the first step towards recovery—she admitted she was powerless. Maybe if she comes this way again, she will not have to go through the same pain and loneliness.

In 1988 I returned to India, first to Bombay to see Paulette. Paulette had left the Missionaries of Charity the year before and had established her own Order. Her mission was to work with the slum dwellers. She and the two young girls who had joined her lived in a house near the Bombay airport. It was stifling hot, and most of the time Paulette was dashing about in just her habit, without anything on her head, exposing her unstyled thatch. She had become a driven woman, and although she was under the authority of the Bishop of Bombay, I felt she was not getting enough direction and was making up her own rules. Now I could see how true were Mother's words about the dangers of "living by the spirit" without spiritual direction. It was frustrating to talk to Paulette; she didn't hear me. I still loved her; I admired her, but I no longer wanted what she had.

During this trip to India I made a spontaneous decision to separate from Mother Teresa. I was uncomfortable with my compulsion to see her all the time; it didn't feel healthy. I felt I was far too dependent on her, and in order to find my own path, I needed to detach myself. So just before leaving Calcutta, I blurted out, "Mother, I will not be coming here any more."

She was surprised by my sudden declaration and, of course, wanted to know why. Unsure of myself or my reasons, I fished around for something to say and eventually pronounced that I felt that somehow I was looking for her to *do* my spirituality for me, that by simply being with her it wouldn't be necessary for me to do the spiritual work myself. When the rich young man walked away, Jesus looked after him sorrowfully, but no matter how much Jesus loved that young man, he couldn't live his life for him; the man had to live it himself. "Mother, I must find my own path."

Mother nodded her head. She didn't say anything and didn't seem at all concerned. There was wisdom in her silence; she was seeing a bigger picture than I could see. I went on, "Well, Mother, this is it. I'm going," and my eyes filled with tears. She took pity.

"Wait a minute."

She dashed off through the curtained alcove behind her and came back with a Miraculous Medal on a silver chain. She called to a sister passing by and asked her to put it around my neck, and then she stood back to admire the effect. Once again I made a motion to leave, and once again she held me back and disappeared into the office. This time she returned with a wooden rosary in a round transparent plastic box. When I opened it, an exotic scent wafted up. The rosary was made from sandalwood and, as the beads passed through my fingers and the subtle smell was released, I thought of incense rising to the Lord. Mother was delighted at my obvious pleasure. I asked her to bless me and lowered my head. Placing both hands on the top of my head, she said her favorite phrase, "Keep the joy of loving Jesus in your heart and spread it to all you meet."

That was it. I went downstairs, turned around, waved to Mother on the balcony and left. As I walked down Rippon Street, I was crying. After the tears, I wasn't sure if I felt free, but I did feel I'd taken a big step.

Six months later, I read in the papers that Mother was in New York, and a great longing to see her washed over me. I resisted, but finally I called the convent in the South Bronx. I was told there would be Professions the next day.

As Mother passed by me after the ceremony, I very softly called, "Mother."

She looked up and exclaimed, "Lorna!"

I was finished, all resistance gone.

"Go to the convent and wait for me," she said.

I left the church and walked around the corner to the convent. Half an hour later she came in. She entered the parlor and extended both hands, into which I surrendered mine.

"Mother, I know I said I wouldn't be visiting you again, but . . ."

She waved aside my protestations as though it had all been a thoroughly ridiculous idea in the first place, but something she had allowed me to go through.

"Don't say any more. I want to see you. I want to see you every time I come to New York; I want you to write to me, and I want to see you in Calcutta."

There was nothing to say. Why could I still not quite believe she loved me? What was wrong with me that I doubted it? The following day she was leaving for Washington but asked me to see her when she returned. I called the South Bronx the next week. "Mother, when may I come?"

"Any time, just come."

A few hours later I was with her in the chapel in the house on 145th Street. Mother sat on a low stool while I sat on the floor at her feet. Although only six months had passed since I had been in Calcutta, something in me had shifted again. I felt I could talk to her with greater ease. I leant against her knees. Her rosary was lying in her lap. I had to ask.

"Mother, do you love me?"

She looked at me, startled by the straightforwardness of my question. "Yes, of course I love you. I love you like I love everyone and . . ."

"No, no, Mother. I don't want to be like everyone for you. Do you love me?"

Mother was quite unaccustomed to this sort of direct confrontation about feelings, and I could sense her reluctance, but realizing I was not going to let it go, she said, "You're a child of God and I love God in you. You're one of the family."

"No, Mother." I pressed on, "I want more from you.

When you see me, is it the same as when you see everyone else? Do I matter in a special way to you? Do you love me?" My hands, clasped together in her lap, implored her. She covered my hands with hers.

"Yes, I love you."

"I love you too, Mother."

I felt I had overcome a childhood fear; I had dared to ask for something important, and it had been given.

Yet another trip to India

In September, 1989, I was having lunch with friends when one of them asked, "Did you hear the news about Mother Teresa?" I felt the hairs on my head stand up on end and my blood turn to ice. "What news?"

"You don't know? She was rushed to the hospital in Calcutta. She had a heart attack." I pushed back from the table, made a beeline for the telephone and called the convent in the South Bronx. Sister Dominga answered and confirmed the news. Yes, Mother had been taken ill and was in the hospital; it wasn't known if it was a heart attack, but she seemed to be all right.

I wanted to go to Calcutta immediately. Memories of not getting home in time to see either my father or mother before they died welled up, but I thought to go to Calcutta now would be pointless; there would be so many others there that my presence would only add to the confusion. Sister Dominga had said the most helpful thing I could do was to pray.

I called the South Bronx every day to inquire about her condition. Some days she was stable, and other days she had a fever. I confessed my feelings of anxiety to Sister Frederick, who had been with Mother for years and was close to her, and I asked her if she were going to Calcutta. "No," she said. She seemed very accepting of Mother's illness, "God has His plan, and we all have our own jobs to fulfill that plan."

Mother got worse. She developed a bad infection after a

temporary pacemaker was attached. A specialist was flown over from America to attend her. I called Sister Frederick only to discover she had been summoned to Calcutta. A call to Ellen temporarily allayed my feelings of panic; she said there is no separation in Heaven, and if we really listen to one another, there's no separation here either. The best thing I could do for Mother and for all of mankind was to live the life I'd been given.

Mother improved and was released from the hospital. A few days later she relapsed. I embarked for Calcutta.

As I stepped out of the plane and walked down the gangway to the tarmac, I paused to inhale the aroma of India, pungent, exotic, unique. Once again I was a courier and traveling with boxes of supplies. Two sisters were at the airport to meet me in the ambulance, which served to transport not only patients but anything else. Within an hour, I was in the Mother House.

I went straight to the chapel where I had been told I would find Sister Priscilla. She had been the Superior in the Bronx the first time I returned from Calcutta and, a few years later, had been called back to India. I went up the familiar stone staircase and found her busy around the altar arranging the flowers that kept pouring in from well-wishers all the world over. She broke from her task and greeted me. "Oh, I'm so glad to see you. Mother was asking after you this morning and wanting to know if you had arrived. She's anxious to see you. It will make her so happy. Sister Shanti and Sister Monica will be going to the hospital in the afternoon, and you should go with them."

After lunch and a nap, I joined Sister Shanti and Sister Monica. At the hospital we walked down several corridors to the intensive care section where a nurses' station monitored a semi-circle of private rooms. Sister Shanti pulled aside the long white curtain covering one of the doors, and I entered Mother's room.

She was sitting up in bed, and when she saw me, she held out both arms. I instantly bowed my head for her blessing. Tears welled up and I couldn't speak. I held her hands. At last I found my voice, and I asked how she was feeling; she quickly brushed away talk of herself and instead told me how kind everyone was and how wonderful they were being. She had been provided with the best possible care—all the treatment had been donated. I noticed the surprise in her voice, as though she couldn't quite believe she was the recipient of so much benevolence.

In one corner of the room stood a table supporting a tabernacle and a small, red candle. The table was covered with a white cloth, and on the wall was a banner someone had made for Mother; on it was embroidered a crucifix and the usual **I Thirst**.

The sisters were telling Mother what was happening at the Mother House, who had called, and other odd tidbits. They were interrupted by a young priest who arrived to say Mass. The table at the foot of the bed was quickly converted into an altar, and, out of an intriguing small black box, the sisters produced all the necessary items for the Mass. Mother saw me looking at it and said, "Isn't it remarkable how God always provides! Someone gave us that box as a gift just recently. It's the first time we've had need of such a thing, and it's perfect." I could see she was enchanted with it.

The priest stood at the foot of the bed; Sister Shanti stood on Mother's left; Sister Monica and I on her right. Being able to share in this intimate Mass with Mother was not lost on me, and I felt an immense gratitude as we made the Sign of the Cross to begin. During the offertory, Mother pushed herself forward off her pillows in order to show full reverence to her Beloved.

When the time came to receive Communion, the priest came around the side of the bed to Mother; I moaned inwardly as I watched him dip the host in the wine and offer it to her. She lowered her head to pray. Next he turned to me.

Oh God, no, not here. Please don't let me have to make a fuss here about the wine, not with the saint of the world just a foot away from me in her sick bed. But then, in a flash, I remembered where I had come from and all those who had helped me. I reminded myself of my unconditional commitment to sobriety no matter what circumstances I found myself in or with whom. I was still an alcoholic even in this privileged situation. The priest had already dipped the host in the chalice of wine and was holding it up for me to take onto my tongue. I felt confused and didn't remember to say, "No sacred blood" or "Only one species please." Instead I stammered out, "No wine."

The poor young man, who was nervous anyway, celebrating Mass for bed-ridden Mother Teresa, looked confused, so I prodded Sister Monica to take the host. Then, as he turned to go away, I said, "I do want Communion, but please don't dip the host in the wine."

By this time I had thoroughly disrupted Mother's devotions, and she was watching the entire exchange. I received Communion.

As I stood there feeling clumsy and shaken, Mother reached across the bed covers and squeezing my hand whispered, "Don't worry, you did well. You must continue to protect your precious gift."

On the way back to the Mother House, the sisters filled me in on the events leading to Mother's hospitalization. "We almost lost her," Sister Shanti said, "she was unconscious

236 · *The Camel Knows the Way*

several times, and we really thought she would die." Sister Monica said Mother's illness had produced a miracle in India because Hindus, Muslims, Jains, Jews, Christians, Buddhists—everyone was praying for her.

"Everyone feels Mother belongs to them," she said. The outpouring of love and concern was something they had never known. The telephone rang endlessly. Mountains of flowers, cards and telegrams arrived. Everywhere people were united in this common concern, and all over the world people were bombarding the gates of Heaven with prayers for her recovery. They told me of the extraordinary things people offered. One man came to the Mother House and said, "I am poor, I have nothing, but I am young and healthy; if the Mother needs any part of my body, I will willingly give it for her."

Three days later Mother came home. I saw her at Adoration. No longer able to get up and down from the floor, she sat on a straw stool. She didn't come for early prayers the next morning but was there at Mass. I was alarmed; I thought she looked awful, and I could tell from her expression that she was uncomfortable. Although Mother thrived on having people around, she also needed time alone, and since I would be in India six weeks and had never seen anything of the country besides Calcutta and Bombay, I decided at last to be a tourist.

I visited the Missionaries of Charity centers in Lucknow, Delhi and Hyderabad. When I arrived at the home for the destitute in Hyderabad, I found an old man sitting outside under a tree. He was freezing. His entire body was cold, and he had a look of death. He sat in his wet shirt and pants, his hollow eyes staring at me. If he had warm clothes, food and a bed, he might make it. I tried to get him to come inside, but all he wanted was a cigarette.

I visited the wards and saw what I had seen so many times—the broken bodies of men and women brought in from the streets, the wasted and the dying. There was no getting used to it. I splurged on a strand of pearls.

From Hyderabad I went to Delhi and visited the Taj Mahal—it's absolutely breathtaking, no picture does it justice. From there I booked myself a train passage to the holy city of Varanasi. The train was due to depart the station at 2 pm and actually pulled out a few minutes after two. I remarked to the woman sitting next to me how extraordinary it was for the train to be departing so close to the scheduled time.

"This is yesterday's train," she replied.

Located on the Ganges, Varanasi is a city where every religious Hindu hopes to die. I found it oppressive yet fascinating. I watched for hours as bodies, wrapped in white gauzy material like chrysalis, burned simultaneously on the funeral pyres at the edge of Holy Mother Ganges only to be replaced by the next lot of bodies—their ashes then strewn onto the surface of the sacred water.

One morning I paid a boatman to take me into the middle of the river so that I could watch the sun rise over the Ganges. I was huddled in the boat wearing a coat and wrapped in a heavy shawl to stay warm in the bitter cold, and I shuddered to see men and women completely submerging themselves in the river as a ritualistic cleansing. Afterwards the faithful stood on the shore praying, their sodden clothes clinging to them. I didn't know if their faith protected them from feeling cold or if they were trying to hasten their own demise.

My love and thirst for the life of Christ had led me inevitably, I feel, to Buddhism with its emphasis on compassion and karma—just another word for reaping and sowing. For many years I had wanted to visit Bodh Gaya where the Buddha received his enlightenment. So from Varanasi I took a train to Bodh Gaya and, while there, sat a ten-day silent meditation retreat. It was there I felt the need for a more extended time of silence and decided to sit a three-month retreat later that year in Massachusetts.

When I returned to Calcutta, Mother looked much better, although she was still confined to the house. I gave her news of the sisters in Lucknow, in Delhi and in Hyderabad. She was delighted I'd seen the Taj Mahal, and I even told her about my pearl splurge although I didn't say a word about the retreat. I remembered an earlier incident when she was in America and I had told her I was going on retreat. She was pleased and wanted to know what sort it was.

"Mother, it's a Buddhist retreat."

"Jesus is not enough for you?" was her fast retort.

We were sitting on the bench outside the office and, unless one was locked away in a room with Mother, it was nigh impossible to spend any length of uninterrupted time with her. There was always something to be attended to: someone wanting something, a phone call, a document to be signed. She said how tired she was of always signing, signing, signing, but then the other day she had counted the number of letters that made up her signature: there were twenty. She decided every time she put her signature on a document, **God bless you, M. Teresa, M.C.**, it was twenty acts of love. Since then, she said, signing had become a prayer instead of a chore.

We talked a little while longer; then it was time for Adoration. Mother had discarded her straw stool; she sat on the floor like everyone else. Adoration finished, and I had the chapel to myself. I moved to a corner of the room to meditate, and a while later I heard someone turn the lights off. When I opened my eyes, it was quite dark, and as I left the chapel, I could see a lone white figure looking over the balcony into the parlor. I realized it was Mother—a queen walking the ramparts of her castle, checking everything was in order. It was she who had turned off the lights. It was odd to see her alone in a house of three hundred women. Not wanting to startle her, I very softly said, "Hello Mother." She jumped anyway.

"Oh, Lorna. Where did you come from? I was looking into the parlor down there, and I thought that was you." I saw where she was pointing. It was at the back of one of the very young volunteers who had her blonde hair in a braid. I said, "Mother, either you're very kind or you have dreadful eyesight. I'm ancient compared to her."

"Nonsense, you look extremely young and, besides, you're full of light. The spirit of God is upon you."

Feeling slightly embarrassed at her pronouncement and wanting her to stop, I replied, "Thank you, Mother, thank you."

"No, it's true; you have changed so much since the first time I saw you, remember? The nail polish. You are so beautiful now." And then, ever practical, "Where are your sandals? Put them on. It's cold here."

"Mother, I'm all right."

"No, no, you must put your sandals on. Where are they? You'll catch cold." I knew there would be no more talking to her until I put my sandals on.

"Those are your sandals? So big!"

"I have big feet Mother."

Sister Xavier was passing. Mother stopped her and asked if she knew me. I said, "Sister, you probably don't remember me, but back in 1981 I came to visit you with Brother Christos at Shanti Nagar."

"Oh, forgive me, I don't remember. We had so many visitors, you understand?"

"Yes, yes, I quite understand."

Mother suddenly wanted to know if I had a crucifix. Not waiting for an answer, she turned to Sister Xavier, "Sister, please go and find Lorna a crucifix, a good one."

The obedience of the Missionaries of Charity is something to witness. Sister Xavier had obviously been on her way somewhere when Mother stopped her, but as soon as Mother asked her to do something, she cheerfully and eagerly went off in the opposite direction to carry out Mother's wishes. A few minutes later she returned with a small crucifix, the classic type carried by a Religious—a metal corpus nailed to a black cross and held within a larger metal cross. It was perfect. Mother was pleased. She kissed it and passed it to me. I was thrilled to have such a beautiful and meaningful gift from Mother. I asked her if I might see the crucifix she carried; she promptly unhooked it from the cord around her waist, kissed it and placed it lovingly into my hands. The metal figure of Christ was smooth and worn from all the kisses and the rubbing against her garments. Mother said, "I've had that crucifix for over fifty years." I knew without asking it was her only possession.

Mother's relationship with material possessions was very simple and yet extraordinary in its simplicity. I was reminded of a time I was in Calcutta in 1984 shortly after she had received the Order of Merit from the Queen. I was congratulating her and said I had seen pictures of her in a magazine, wearing her old navy-blue cardigan receiving her medal. She said how very nice the Queen was—"a lovely lady, and she gave me such a nice medal. Go and see it, it's on the Blessed Virgin."

I went into the chapel, and around the neck of the statue was a fabulously crafted golden badge, with red and blue enamel, surmounted by a crown. It had been fastened with a length of fraying ribbon and a whacking great safety pin. The Order of Merit is an unusual and highly prestigious honor given as the sole prerogative of the British monarch, but for Mother it neither added nor took away attention from her purpose.

The following afternoon I was trying to spend time with Mother and had been with her a mere five minutes when in came a troupe of French pilgrims. They were going around India reciting the Rosary. There must have been two hundred of them, and they were only part of a much larger group, they told us. My chance of an intimate chat with Mother went out the window. The pilgrims crowded around her, snapping their cameras and trying to kiss her. Mother was fending them off very nicely, avoiding their hugs and kisses.

"Mother has only recently returned from the hospital. Please be careful with her." I implored them. But they wanted to be with her; they wanted to touch her. I could understand; I felt that way too. She was like a rock star of the spiritual world. They were swarming all over the balcony and the yard. Mother said Adoration would be starting soon and they should go into the chapel. Adoration was particularly sweet; the pilgrims responded to the Hail Mary's in French and sang in French between each decade.

When the prayers were over and the Blessed Sacrament had been put away, Mother addressed the group. She stood, they sat. But even standing she didn't look much taller than they—a diminutive figure in a sea of upturned faces. She said the same simple things she always said about prayer and Mass and keeping a relationship with the Blessed Mother. Some of her fans held miniature tape recorders to catch every word she spoke. When she'd finished her short speech, she all but ran from the chapel so as not to be inundated by the group again.

As she passed me she said, "I'm sorry; come tomorrow at three and we'll talk."

When I arrived the following day just before 3 pm, there were rows of chairs set up in the courtyard. Sister Shanti explained that a French orchestra was due there any minute to play for the sisters. No sooner had she spoken than the musicians came piling in with their instruments and music stands. All the sisters had been summoned; the balconies overlooking the courtyard were full. I can't remember what was played; it was sacred music, and it delighted Mother no end. When the twenty-minute concert was over, the members of the orchestra came upstairs and filed passed Mother. The men bowed and kissed her hand while the women curtsied and did the same.

The musicians left. Mother and I had just sat down when a bishop from South Dakota showed up. He was quite beside himself to meet Mother Teresa and asked if he could say Mass in the chapel.

"Yes, of course," was her immediate response. Nothing was as important to Mother as attending Mass, so we all went into the chapel. Mass over, the bishop wanted to talk with Mother for a while, she looked at me apologetically.

"Mother, please don't worry, it's not important. We'll visit some other time when God sees fit."

"When are you leaving Calcutta?"

"I leave tomorrow evening."

"So soon? I didn't realize you were leaving so soon. After Mass tomorrow we will definitely talk; I promise."

The next morning after Mass, Mother instructed me to go into the sacristy where we wouldn't be interrupted. She had to have her breakfast and had breakfast sent to me; a postulant brought in a tray with a hard-boiled egg, a banana, bread and tea.

Mother came. She bolted both doors to the little room so we couldn't be disturbed and sat down at the table with me. Finally! I hadn't anything I really wanted to say. I just wanted to be with her for a while.

I looked into that dear face with its deep wrinkles and impish eyes; she was always pulling faces and loved to laugh—not a throw-your-head-back laugh, but a soft amused chortle. I asked her if she looked like her own mother. "I don't know. It's been so many years and, besides, I never look at myself in a mirror, and I don't really know what I look like."

I knew nuns tried to temper vanity, but to think that, in this day and age, a woman didn't know what she looked like was astonishing. What freedom Mother had. I asked her many questions, especially one I had wondered about since we first met.

"Mother, why do you not let people kiss you?"

"I belong only to Jesus. Jesus is my spouse and my kisses are for him."

Coming from anyone else it would have sounded ludicrous, if not slightly mental. But from Mother it sounded rational and enviable.

"The last person I kissed was my own mother when I said goodbye to her." I conjured up a picture of Mother Teresa—Agnes, as she then was—eighteen years old, wearing a hat and coat, embracing her mother for the last time on Skopje Railway station in Yugoslavia. What purity, what great love; she had not kissed anyone except babies for over fifty years, and yet she was the very embodiment of love. Then, in a delighted, playful voice, she said, "When I meet the Holy Father, he is so tall, you know, he kisses me on the top of my head."

Sitting at the table with Mother, I felt we were two dear friends locked away having a chat. We were not talking about anything particularly earthshaking or noteworthy. We were just being together and enjoying each other's company.

It was time to go. We unbolted the door of the sacristy and emerged. As we walked past the chapel, we genuflected together. Mother called to Sister Priscilla, who handed me a large package of letters to be delivered in the States. Once again I asked Mother for her blessing.

"Keep the joy of loving Jesus in your heart and spread it to all you meet."

My Dark Night

We met shortly before my mother died. I had been minimally aware of him on the far reaches of my universe, but within weeks of her death, he came toward me like a meteorite crashing into my immediate orbit. And I welcomed his intensity.

The relationship lasted four years, and then it was over. It had been wonderful and not wonderful, satisfying and limiting, painful and joyful. I loved him and knew, on a level I was unable to fathom, we were strangely connected. But I began to feel something was suffocating my spirit, that a light in me was being extinguished. Our union became my convenient excuse, and I wanted out. Once the notion of parting was in my heart and out of my mouth, the love affair frayed beyond repair. Together we chose a date to go our separate ways. The closer we got to that day, the lighter I began to feel.

"Ending this relationship so abruptly will cause you a lot of pain," a friend warned. "Yes, yes, I know. I know it will be painful for a while," I agreed, "but I'm not scared of a little pain." I had been sober fifteen years and was sure I had a strong spiritual foundation. I was forty-five, had buried both parents, been married, divorced, landed and lost jobs and sundry lovers. Life had happened. I thought the pain of ending this love affair would move through all the usual stages; it would stay for a while, then go. I thought I could dictate to my heart. But I was blind to the depth of my feelings and to the strength of my attachment.

Almost immediately after we parted, I felt only terror. I had a childhood sense of being shut out and banished— I was baffled and frantic to understand what was happening.

When I was in Jerusalem shortly after my father died, I met an old Italian priest who said he believed that while the death of one's father shakes the psyche, it is the death of one's mother that has the more profound impact. Most of us, he felt, do not come into our own emotionally or spiritually until our mother dies. My mother's passing must have sent a signal to supernal realms that it was time for those decayed and rotting parts of my soul to be cut away, as I had cut away Meeta's burned and rotting flesh in order to save her life.

Gradually, gradually I came to know the relationship had not been the cause of my spiritual malady and sense of suffocation. Although I missed him, and often wanted to run back for relief, I knew turning back was useless, that the relief I craved would act only to stall momentarily whatever hellish process I was in. I began to suspect the real purpose of the relationship all along had been to lead me to the edge of this abyss.

I believe that the buildup for this period of my life had accumulated little by little, drop by drop, over countless eons and now was a tidal wave of past karma, unacknowledged feelings and spiritual pride. The relationship had been the last dam holding back the deluge, and when it broke, suddenly, shockingly suddenly, a mighty force was released and thundered down, sweeping me out of my comfort and drowning me in a pain I had never known. All the spiritual tools I had relied on before were now stripped away. It was as if I had been sitting serenely on the beach meditating when the tidal wave came, and the next thing I knew, I was five miles inland, naked on a thorn bush. I had the dreadful feeling of being separated from God. Mass, which had been such a comfort, was now torture. I walked into church, and like a vampire confronted with the cross, I would sting and burn and have to leave. As I toppled further into the abyss, I plunged into subterranean fields of pain, all the pain I had denied in myself as well as the pain I had inflicted on others.

Repeatedly I swept a search light over my past but could not find anything I had done in this life which in any way warranted this magnitude of retribution. Then I would remember that Jesus spoke of karma and said, "As you sow, so shall you reap." He did not add, "unless you die beforehand, and then you can get away with it." I felt this was the harvest of greed, hatred and unkindness, the clearing out of accumulated garbage from my wrongs. I felt my filing cabinet had been jerked open and all the old contents were spilling out—files I had assumed were neatly put away. Try as I might, I could not cram them back into the drawers. This was the very pith of my disease, my soul-sickness, the stuff I drank over. This episode had to be experienced undiluted, and I was unable to distract myself. I had to pass through my own dark night.

Mornings used to represent promise, but for me they now heralded more horror. I would be jolted out of the blessed relief of sleep by a gigantic thud, as though kicked awake by some fiend whose delight it was to summon me. I'd shoot out of bed and attempt to meditate, but meditation was impossible—my inner silence too loud and jagged. Or at five in the morning I would be running around the Central Park reservoir. Even in temperatures of eight degrees below zero, it made no difference. I ran. I had to run.

At other times, I would stare into space for hours, unable to move. I would come to—sitting on the edge of the bed with one foot in my pantyhose—only to realize I'd been there for ages. Putting in the other foot seemed like a monumental undertaking.

Several mornings I dressed and headed for the subway. Halfway there, I had to turn around, go home, get undressed, crawl back into bed and pull the covers over my head. I feared that once in the subway station, that same fiend would goad me into jumping in front of the oncoming train.

I could hardly breathe; I could hardly walk. At night, exhausted from trying to keep myself moving forward, I'd collapse into a coma-like sleep. I would occasionally have a glimmer that one day all this would pass.

But even the glimmer diminished. The pain was relentlessness. At times I would be fooled into thinking I was out of the dangerous water wading in shallow surf towards the safety of the beach. Then suddenly a wave would come from behind, knock me over and drag me face down, across stones and rocks, back into the churning waters. There was nothing solid about me. I had no edges, no definition. Formless, I floated in the pain.

The first year-and-a-half took its toll physically—I lost forty pounds. The surgical spiritual paring felt more like slow butchery. One night I was startled awake by a noise outside. I thought I had inconveniently come to while God was in the process of performing open-heart surgery on me. It was a hideous moment. I lay pinned to the bed, unable to move until the agonizing procedure was complete.

Friends fell by the wayside; my dark night had long outlasted their patience. One that didn't leave wrote to me:

> You are indeed luxuriating in the crucible of that spiritual death and resurrection out of which you will surely emerge chastened, purified and triumphant. It's a most indescribable bleeding of purgatory or

hell, which dwells outside of any emotional or psychological reference point we have for our normal periods of painful growth and transition.

I am tempted to say rather sanctimoniously that it's a blessing in disguise. Don't forget you are a prayer of supplication right now, and your silent scream is being heard and answered. Read the twenty-third psalm. You are in the no-man's land of spiritual emptiness and fulfillment that lies beyond therapy, beyond prayer itself. God is with you in it, suffering with you, always, always with the promise and assurance that your resurrection and a new wonderful phase of spiritual development is imminent. And when you emerge, your Easter will be spectacular.

I had another wonderful friend—someone I had met quite by chance as I started my decent into Hell. In agony, every morning I called her; she never told me how to fix it, how to get out of the pain. She never gave me any advice or offered any suggestions; she just said over and over, "Lorna you're doing so well, just remember to breathe."

Others suggested I take anti-depressants, but I knew what was happening to me was spiritual not clinical. And even though I desperately wanted this state to end, I was reluctant to miss any part of it. Drinking had dulled so much of my life; now I wanted to be awake for all my experiences, painful and pleasant alike. I believe the saddest words in the Bible are, ". . . Jesus passed by." (Matt. 20:30) I didn't want any experience to pass me by. "You asked God for something," Mother had said, "and He took you at your word." I had forgotten I had asked God for a Mystical Marriage with Him. Now I hoped He had forgotten too. It's not loving God that is difficult, it's being loved by Him that's not always so jolly.

I went back to India to see Mother. I needed a mother. I desperately needed a mother, and I felt working in Calcutta would help me to get the focus off myself and alleviate the pain. Helping others had always been a great antidote for emotional distress. But this time I was not granted the noble distraction; I could not circumvent the process. Without my having to explain, Mother could tell I was being ravaged by pain and that something inexplicable was happening to me. She made arrangements for me to stay at Shishi Bhavan with the other orphans. It was perfect. For three weeks, I slept on a tiny cot in the dispensary. At night I could hear children coughing and crying. There was an outbreak of a severe fever and some died. But I felt safe there.

One month wove into another and still no relief. I had just been with a saint who had poured love onto me. But not even a saint could penetrate this darkness. I had to wait it out. I had to wait on God.

Later that year I met Mother in New York; she was concerned and asked how I was.

"Mother, it's hell, it's absolute hell," I replied.

"How God must love you," she said in a wondrous tone, "and He wants to be very intimate with you." I looked at her incredulously. "No, no, it's true," she said, "but He is a jealous lover, and He is burning out of your soul *everything* unlike Himself."

"Oh, gee, that's just swell, Mother. If this is the way God expresses His love, who would want it?" I sympathized with Teresa of Avila who said to God, "If this is the way you treat your friends, no wonder you have so few of them."

The pain started to shift. It was the beginning of the next phase. It still had a relentless quality, but at least there was movement, even if it was like dancing with a gorilla—no stopping until he'd had enough. Gradually, very gradually, s.o.m.   24-11-92

My dear Lorna,
        Thank you for your letter
of 9-11-92 - I am sorry for the
delay in answering -
    Do not be afraid - Jesus is
drawing you to Himself on
the Cross - to share in His
Passion - this is but the
kiss of Jesus - a sign that
you have come so
close to Jesus on the
Cross that He can kiss
you - Do not afraid
St. John of the Cross went
through the same trial
he called it " The dark
night of the Soul "
This trial in your life is
a gift of God, do not miss it
Do not stop the beautiful (gift)
God has entrusted to you
Defenetly Jesus loves you
So He wants you to be
His love in action.
    Offer the feelings of
darkness for Peace in the
World. Do not be afraid.
This time is time of Greater Love
    I am praying for you
                    God bless you
                        Mc Teresa

Letter from Mother, 1992

the vise around my soul and heart loosened its grip, and slowly tiny green blades of grass started poking through the wasteland. I spent an evening with friends; as we prepared dinner, I heard something I hadn't heard for a long time—the sound of myself laughing, a high-spirited, fresh laughter, laughter that comes from the spring of life, from newness, from joy.

My dark night lasted four years, and, like an acid trip, I can recall the feelings vividly. I cannot talk about *getting out* of this period. *I* didn't get out of it. God came into the wilderness where I was and led me out. Strangely my emergence from the pain was around the same time I was in the Sinai and the Bedouin abandoned me on the camel. Was it God under those long lashes asking me to trust in Him no matter what? Had it been God softly plodding through the sand carrying me home?

At times I don't know what continually draws me along the spiritual path. Maybe it is a boundless curiosity, an insatiable thirst. But then I wonder, what is the spiritual path? How do I know if I'm even on one? I really have no idea. I have no answers. Sometimes I get a glimpse; I notice perhaps I have more compassion, tolerance and love than I had ten years ago. Then I wonder, "Is this really the spiritual path, or just age mellowing me?" Although I love the transforming adventure, I am also aware that the persistent, self-willed pursuit of the spiritual can pull me off track; like any obsession it, too, can lead to desire. Strong desire in turn can lead to greed, and greed clogs the spiritual arteries, starving the soul.

I became aware that unless my attention continually turns from *my* spiritual journey to *our* spiritual journey, unless I include others in the process of my journey, it will be a dry, withering pursuit. Jesus shared his life and his spiritual process with his disciples, and when the thief crucified with him pleaded, "Remember me, Lord, when you come into your Kingdom," Jesus did not say, "Please don't bother me right now, can't you see I'm busy? I'm involved in a profound spiritual experience, and I don't have time for you." Instead he turned to the stranger and promised, "This day you will be with me in Paradise."

I believe that, unlike the camel, there is no absolute "knowing the way," our journeys can never be fully learned or complete. It is this freedom to search that makes us different—it is the source of our potential agony and passion, our humanity.

I also believe that the greatest form of love is to give another our complete attention. Meditation helps me foster this love and attention. Meditation is, for me, at once simple and difficult—all I have to do is be in the moment, yet my mind flits all over the place. Minor irritations can serve to detonate the most elevated feelings. I can be in the rarified atmosphere of a long meditation retreat when suddenly I find myself lost in judgment. I become distracted by how much a fellow yogi is eating, or perhaps I envy how beautifully another yogi sits. I think, "I'm a dreadful yogi." Or I think, "I'm a great yogi." Or I think, "This is ridiculous, what am I doing here anyway?" Sometimes I know the Kingdom of Heaven is at hand. Other times I wonder if it even exists.

Once, when I was on retreat, Joseph Goldstein, a revered meditation teacher, was giving a talk on impermanence. He said that everything can be going along gloriously and the heart feels uplifted, but come the next day, the next hour, even the next minute, and there can be an onslaught of doubt or fear. We can get annoyed about something minor, and we're baffled. We think we've left out some vital ingredient we had in the mix before, and we cannot figure out what the missing ingredient might be. We blame ourselves when really it's just life performing its ever-changing dance.

Goldstein went on to say he had been an ardent seeker and pilgrim on the spiritual path, and that after many years of searching, he had finally found the answer. He had discovered the truth, the essence, the real meaning of spiritual life, and now he would pass on this truth to us, the gathered yogis.

I sat a little straighter, my mind clear, bright and alert, poised for the transmission of this great and noble insight. I had sought spiritual wisdom around the world; I had sat under the Bodhi tree in Bodh Gaya where the Buddha received his enlightenment. I had kissed the site of the True Cross, bathed in Galilee, prayed at the Western Wall. I had sat in silent meditation for months on end; fasted for forty days; climbed Mount Sinai and spent time in the desert. I had a love affair with Jesus and had claimed my love for Him out loud. I had held the dying and buried the dead. I had hugged lepers and cleaned maggots out of flesh, sat and listened to others' pain—all on the search for truth. At last this teacher was going to give me the answer. And Goldstein said,

"If it's not one thing, it's another."

Saying Thank You

I had had a great run. For fifteen years since leaving Sotheby's, the universe had bountifully provided for my every need and allowed me the freedom to travel. But my money had run out, and I was troubled about my financial situation. During the last year I had often been reminded of a scene in the movie *Gandhi* where a young Englishman says to the Mahatma, "It costs a lot of money to keep you in poverty."

Towards the end of 1996 there were again constant and alarming reports from Calcutta about Mother Teresa's health. She had suffered another heart attack and had to undergo yet another procedure to unclog the arteries of her heart. She was now eighty-six, and there was a very real possibility that she would die. The world held its breath. December came and went. The news bulletins flashed: Mother was getting better, Mother was getting worse. Eventually I was relieved to see an image of her on television; she was in a wheelchair leaving the Calcutta hospital.

One morning, in late January of '97, I went to the South Bronx for Mass with the Missionaries of Charity. Afterwards I spoke to Sister Dominga about Mother's health; she told me Mother was in a lot of pain. Tears filled our eyes.

Once again I wanted to run to Calcutta but sat tight. Mother was still very ill, and I assumed there would be a strict limitation on visitors. And I didn't have the money to go. This particular health crisis of Mother's brought me face-to-face with the truth about my financial situation. It was the first time I was unable to do something I considered important because I couldn't afford to.

I talked to a friend in California about my frustration. He responded immediately, "Lorna, there's no question in my mind: you simply have to go to India to see Mother, and you must go just as soon as you possibly can. You belong there. This is such an important relationship for you *and* for her." He went on, "I would really like to feel connected to Mother Teresa in some way and, since I cannot go to India myself, helping you get there would allow me to feel involved. Let me contribute to your airfare."

With a good portion of the fare paid, my burden was certainly lighter, but I still needed help. With a boldness that comes only from having conviction and a little desperation, I reached out. Heaven responded, friends rallied, and I was given enough to cover the trip.

I left New York for Calcutta on February 16, 1997. This was the eighth time I had made the journey. I wanted *this* trip, however, to be different from the others. I had always gone to Mother to receive something from her—her love, her blessing, or just her presence. This time I wanted to give her the gesture of traveling thousands of miles simply to tell her I loved her and to thank her for being in my life.

Since my visit coincided with the Missionaries of Charity's General Chapter, I wasn't sure I'd be able to see her. The Chapter convenes only once every six years and is the time when the Regionals and Delegates gather in Calcutta to decide new policy and discuss the business of the Order. This was a particularly momentous Chapter. Mother Teresa was the foundress of the Missionaries of Charity and now, after almost fifty years, she was stepping down, and a new Mother General was to be elected.

Chapter meetings are usually held in a quiet spot just outside Calcutta, but because of Mother's fragile health, it was decided that she should stay at home, and therefore the Chapter would meet at the Mother House. Postulants, aspirants and most of the novices, who usually lived there, were transferred to another convent in the city to make room for the influx of sisters arriving from all over the world. The Mother House was closed to outsiders.

I arrived in Calcutta early in the morning. It had been four years since I was last there. Two figures in the familiar white and blue sari were waiting for me; Sister Dominga must have called ahead. I bounded over to them. Sister Priscilla had dispatched Sisters Annie and Brunette to collect me. Sister Brunette quickly assured me.

"Of course you'll see Mother!"

We made the ride into the city in a small, noisy bus with minimal suspension. It was the same congested Calcutta but with some noticeable changes. Calcutta was sprucing up. Gone were the hundreds of vendors who plied their wares on the sidewalks, forcing pedestrians into the roads. Gone, too, were the cows—transported to country pastures. Traffic lights had been installed and, even more incredibly, motorists obeyed them!

Inside the Mother House, it was unusually quiet. There were wooden doors I had not noticed before, closing the entrance to the yard. I suppose I hadn't noticed them because they had always been open. Tacked on the doors was a handwritten sign: **PRIVATE. NO VISITORS ALLOWED BEYOND THIS POINT. CHAPTER IN SESSION.**

My companions asked me to wait and disappeared behind the doors. Within minutes Sister Brunette returned and beckoned to me saying that Sister Priscilla was waiting for me in Mother's room. I couldn't believe it. I thought I'd have to wait days, perhaps only have a moment with Mother after Mass one morning, but now, right now! And in her room! It was all so fast.

"I've just got off the plane. I look such a mess." I was suddenly nervous—not really about how I looked, but I didn't know how Mother would look or how she would be. I crossed the yard. A brand new flight of metal stairs led up to Mother's room. I had never before been in Mother's room. I had never even been behind the curtains that separated the convent areas of the house from those where visitors were allowed.

At the top of the stairs, a smiling Sister Priscilla said a quick hello as though I'd just arrived from around the corner. She said Mother was feeling better and that it would cheer her up enormously to see me; now was the perfect time. Since Mother tired easily, she asked me to keep my visit brief. We stepped into the room. Mother was seated at her desk, bent over and still signing the endless papers. Sister Priscilla said, "Mother, look who's here."

Mother looked up at me with a puzzled face; then, after a moment or two, her face lit up and she extended her arms.

"How wonderful! What a surprise! What are you doing in Calcutta? Sit. Sit," and she pointed to the stool crammed between the desk and a small bookcase.

"Mother, I understand you're looking for a new Mother General. Well, here I am!"

"Oh, so you want to be Mother General? That's very good. You would make a good Mother General. How are you?"

"Mother, I'm very, very well, and I'm incredibly happy to be here and to be able to see you. How are you?"

"I'm fine. Much better, thank God."

I could see she was not fine. I could see the pain in her

face and the oxygen tank in the corner of the room. She was pale and looked worn out. My dearest Mother. All I had wanted to say seemed inappropriate. It was not the right time to engage in any heavy pronouncements. I chatted breezily for a little longer; she gestured toward a framed letter on the wall. It was from President Clinton conferring on her honorary citizenship in the United States. Mother had a strong affection for the United States and was quite chuffed with her citizenship. I admired the letter and stood to leave. I said I would see her again soon.

She took my hands and said, "All for Jesus. All for Jesus. Please come for Mass."

I cast a backward glance. I could see she had immediately returned to her work. My eyes quickly took in the rest of the room. It was approximately nine feet by seven feet and extremely simple. On the right was an iron bedstead, a white spread covering it; on the left, her desk—a plain, wooden desk with a crucifix and small statue of the Blessed Virgin on it. On the wall above the desk, was a crown of thorns. Mother sat on an old-fashioned office chair upholstered in worn pinkish-colored leather. There was only a small space between the back of the chair and the bed. I knew the chair was a recent addition, a concession to her fragility. She, like all Missionaries of Charity, usually sat on a backless wooden stool or bench. This tiny room with its few scraps of furniture was where she worked and laid her head to rest at night.

The family was gathered. One of the unexpected gifts of being in Calcutta during the Chapter was seeing so many sisters I had met over the years in Delhi, Bombay, Pondicherry, Lucknow, Hyderabad and other parts of the world—Cairo, London, Rome, Amman, Gaza—sisters I never expected to see again. Even Sister Henrietta, who had greeted me at the Mother House on my first visit, was there.

I was thrilled to see her. Since 1981 she had been stationed in different places in Africa and in Australia.

Sisters Nirmala and Francita were in the hospital with a fever. I visited them several times. They were over the worst and were due to be released within a few days. Sister Nirmala had been raised a Hindu and had converted to Catholicism to the horror of her Brahmin family. She had joined the Missionaries of Charity shortly after her conversion and was the first Superior of the Contemplative branch in New York. Sister Francita was American; I had bumped into her one afternoon while she and another sister were waiting for a bus in the Port Authority Bus Terminal in New York. Concerned for their safety, I had asked them to wait in my nearby apartment, and subsequently we became friends.

I was permitted into the Mother House every day for Mass; it was a great privilege. Mother was there; she no longer sat on the floor or a straw stool; she was in a wheelchair. Although she was capable of walking, she was not steady on her feet and had fallen several times. Sitting next to her every morning in the chapel was a dying Sister Agnes. Sister Agnes had been a student at the Loretto convent where Mother taught (before leaving and establishing the Missionaries of Charity) and had been the first to join Mother. Now cancer was killing her. She was carried into the chapel, a dark purple shawl around her shoulders. She sat propped against the wall, tiny, quiet and suffering.

One morning Sister Andrea asked me if I would bring my camera to Mass the next day. The sisters wanted pictures of Mother and Sister Agnes together. I was surprised. I knew the taking of pictures in the Mother House was frowned upon; in fact, there were a few notices posted, asking visitors not to. I protested, saying Mother would be angry if I took pictures, especially during Mass. Why didn't *she* take the pictures? "Oh no," she said, "I couldn't possibly!"

"Oh, I suppose it's all right if Mother is annoyed with *me*."

The following morning, after Mother and Sister Agnes had received Communion and were praying, Sister Andrea indicated that I should now take the pictures. Stealthily I crouched in front of them and snapped a few. I was creeping back to my place when Sister Brunette caught my arm and whispered, "Take more. Take as many as you can."

I was nervous; what if Mother should open her eyes and see me darting about? Then Sister Andrea wanted more photographs. The "first group" were there. They were sisters who, just out of school, had joined Mother; now they were in their sixties and seventies. After the Chapter they would again disperse all over the world, unlikely ever to be together again.

After Mass I was asked would I please take a group photograph? I was honored. They all stood in the chapel in front of the statue of the Blessed Virgin. Sister Agnes sat beside Mother, who was none too happy about all the fuss, especially as sisters kept dashing forward to "arrange" her for the historic photo.

After that I saw Mother every day but only to greet her in passing as she was wheeled back to her room after Mass. Every day she looked better. One morning Sister Monica stopped me as I was leaving and said Mother would like to see me, and could I come back later?

I returned to the Mother House at 10 am. I waited in the quietness of the house until Mother came out. We sat outside the chapel, she in her wheelchair, me on the bench, our knees touching. She was alert and in a talkative mood. We were alone, it was the perfect moment. I gently took her hands in mine and leaned into her lap, that lap of soft white cotton laundered countless times in an old tin bucket. And, in a reversal of a previous time in the South Bronx, I slowly said:

"Mother, I came to Calcutta *just* to see you. I've been able to come because of the love and generosity of friends. I've come to bring you their love and good wishes and to tell you how much *I* love you. You are so dear and so precious to me. I am grateful to have you in my life. I feel blessed that God put us in the world at the same time and that I found you."

I could hardly speak because of my emotions, but I was determined not to miss my chance. I pressed on, "What a dear, dear mother you have been to me, and I simply want to thank you from the bottom of my heart for all you have given me and all that you have shown me."

Mother held my eyes with hers. The tears spilled down my cheeks. She spoke, but I couldn't register what she was saying. All that registered was her look, a look of unutterable sweetness and love. That dear face, the face of Jesus.

We sat for a little while just holding hands. I bent my head for her blessing and Mother softly said, "I don't pray for you; I just thank God for you."

Brimming over with irrepressible love and gratitude, I took my leave.

Full Circle

Just as my camel, Bob Marley, intuitively knew his path through the Sinai, I too somehow knew that it was time for me to chart a course—to unload cargo I had carried for decades. I stopped in London on my way back to New York in order to close some childhood chapters.

I went to see the house where I'd grown up and discovered it was now the staff annex for a nearby motel. The house was shabby and forlorn; paint was peeling off the window frames and the front door. Nonetheless, as I looked through the letterbox, I saw again my mother wearing a floral apron, going down the hall into the kitchen. I saw the glorious garden my father had tended with such care, not the asphalt car park that was now in its place. I shut my eyes and conjured the smells of the freshly mowed grass, the pears squashed on the garden path, the sound of the kitchen door closing, the taste of the mint sprinkled on my mother's new potatoes. I felt a sadness at the passing, but my memories would *not* pass.

I returned to Gumley House, the cradle of my spiritual longings. No longer a convent school, it was now a school run by the local council. The original old house was the same, but many new buildings had been added, eliminating the beautiful park that had once been our playground. The chapel where I had made my First Holy Communion was now a library. The old statues were gone. Much of the highly polished wood had been painted over, and the beautiful stairs were now covered in linoleum. The black-and-white marble squares in the entrance hall were dulled with age—there were no young sisters on their hands and knees polishing them. The few nuns remaining had discarded their black habits long ago, the only thing distinguishing them as Religious was the emblem of their order worn on a chain around their neck. I would never need to revisit this place; I knew I was saying a final goodbye. But I would always be able to hear the echo of Mother Agnes' shoes walking down the marble halls and to smell the furniture polish on the wood balustrade. In my memory, Linda and I would always be eight years old and running up the stairs in our school uniforms. The serenity of the old house would always be with me.

Back in New York, my financial situation had not changed. I was still broke. I did all sorts of odd jobs to keep afloat; I even filled in as a doorman at an apartment building. But I had to face the fact that another part of my journey had come full circle. My unstructured life was over, and it was time to change. My skills were out of date; I didn't understand computers, and I didn't know where to look for a job. I asked a friend what I should do. She thought I would be well suited for special events planning. Even though I knew nothing about it, nor did I know anyone in the field, I was open to all suggestions. Somewhere wheels were turning. Within a week, I received a call from someone looking for help in his office. He was a producer of special events. Was I interested? With some apprehension, but with a sense of excitement and adventure, I returned to the world of nine-to-five, pantyhose, and two weeks' vacation a year.

June '97

Much to everyone's surprise, Mother recovered to such an extent that in less than four months, after saying good-bye for what I believed would be the last time, she was well enough to travel again. She and Sister Nirmala flew to Rome and from there to New York. I was overjoyed to see Mother looking so much better and also to see Sister Nirmala, who had been elected the new Mother General.

Because of the numbers of people wanting to see Mother, I was even more grateful I had made my last trip to Calcutta. If I had not gone, I might not have had any time with her at all. I was able to greet her after Mass in the mornings and saw flashes of her on the nightly news. One evening the TV news ran a story on Princess Diana's visit to Mother. The next morning after Mass, I teased her, "So you're hanging out with royalty now!"

"Oh, yes. When I was in London, the Princess took me to her home, and now she has come to mine."

The day Mother left New York to return to India, I asked for time off from work to go to the South Bronx and say goodbye.

As I turned the corner on 145th Street, I saw police cars and a small crowd. I rang the convent doorbell and was shown into the parlor to wait. After a while the community gathered in the chapel for the prayers the Missionaries of Charity recite before a journey. Mother was then wheeled down the narrow hallway to the front door. There were so many sisters I couldn't get to her, but she saw me and said, "I'm so glad you came."

As she emerged onto the street, the crowd cheered and surged forward to touch her. The police held them back, but Mother reached out her hand; it was seized, eagerly shaken and kissed by well-wishers. She got in the front seat of the car, which had been provided with a special support for her back. Besides the usual commotion of Missionaries of Charity on the move, this time there were police cars with their flashing lights; there were flashing cameras and people calling out to Mother. Almost all the sisters were going with her to the airport, some to see her off, others traveling with her to India.

I stood near the driver's seat of Mother's car while he was helping sisters load boxes. Sister Nirmala, who was sitting in the back, beckoned to me and asked me to fasten Mother's seat belt. As I leaned over the driver's seat and pulled the strap around her to close the buckle into place, an odd thing happened. In the middle of all the commotion, Mother and I were somehow secluded—caught in a bubble. The world outside seemed to stop, the noise muted, the activity faded into the background. We were alone together in one last blessed connection.

I was on my knees bent over her, and she could see I was close to tears. She held my arm and whispered, "How are you?"

I whispered back, "I'm well, Mother. I'm so grateful to have seen you."

"I'm sorry we didn't spend any time together, but I'm so happy you came to say goodbye. When will you come to Calcutta again?"

"Soon, God willing. I love you."

"If I open a house in China, you come!"

And that was all. It was my purest moment with Mother. All too soon the world closed in again. I backed out of the car, the driver sat in his seat, and amidst much waving and cheering, Mother's car pulled away.

I never really knew what it is about Mother that affects so many people. After all, she is a human being, a little old lady, and she has her foibles. But in that thirty-second encounter I knew why it is I can't get enough of her. It's because she's so close to Jesus. She embodies the love of God, and that love is completely irresistible. She is nothing but that love. That's all she is.

I stood and waited for the last of the entourage to disappear at the end of the street before making my way back into the convent and the chapel. The house was quiet; only a few sisters had stayed behind. A postulant was fussing around the altar, laying out new linen and generally tidying up; another was on her knees in front of the tabernacle. Soon they left, and I was there by myself, sitting on the linoleum floor and staring at the words **I Thirst** on the wall, while the white muslin curtains fluttered in the breeze on a perfect June afternoon.

Mother Teresa died September 5, 1997.

Glossary

Acha	Good.
Ayah	Female servant.
Baksheesh	Alms.
Bangla	Illegal alcoholic brew.
Bidis	Cigarettes hand rolled in a leaf.
Barfi	Bengali nougat.
Charpoy	Bed made with rope.
Chula	Clay stove.
Dal	Chick pea soup eaten with rice.
Djellaba	Arab robe.
Gunda	Crook.
Inro	Japanese—a small compartmentalized box (usually lacquer), used for carrying snuff and medicines.
Kadi cloth	Homespun cloth.
Kali	Goddess of destruction and benevolent mother.
Kohl	A black medicinal preparation used as a cosmetic around the eyes.
Longhi	Length of fabric worn by men wrapped around lower half of the body.
Namaskar	Greeting–peace.
Paise	Small coin.
Pan	Addictive substance.
Roti	Flat pancake.
Sabra	Female Israeli soldier.
Wallah	Male servant.
Zamidar	Landlord.

Mary Turner
266-6283

The
beginning of
wisdom is to call something
by its correct name-
page 95